Vita's Will

Vita's Will

Real Life Lessons about Life, Death & Moving On

Debbie Gisonni

Writers Club Press
San Jose New York Lincoln Shanghai

Vita's Will
Real Life Lessons about Life, Death & Moving On

Writers Club Press
an imprint of iUniverse.com, Inc.

For information address:
iUniverse.com, Inc.
620 North 48th Street, Suite 201
Lincoln, NE 68504-3467
www.iuniverse.com

Cover design by Ewa Gavrielov

Author photo by Abigail Huller

ISBN: 0-595-14204-4

Printed in the United States of America

To Vita, Martha, Tommy and Yolanda, whose inspiring lives made this story possible.

To my husband Joe and my sister Angela, for your unconditional love, undying support and invaluable input.

Contents

Acknowledgements

To all my friends and family who willingly read the many versions along the way, thank you for your time, insight and assistance in creating this book, especially Mike Azzara, Shauna Bergman, Angela Gisonni, Joe Prestipino, Gina Reidy, Coleen Schepis and Pam Walsh.

To Susan Blake, Barbara Courtney, Rebecca Covington, Jenai Lane, Gates McKibbin and Wendy Weir, thank you for your wisdom, friendship and help in awakening my spirit.

To my editor Erin Blackwell, thank you for your patience, expertise and the many thought-provoking hours we spent together.

To my publicity experts, Susan Harrow and Anita Halton, thank you for believing in me and for all your help in making the dream come true.

To Joanne Persico, Sean Fulton and John Familette for my web site, Ewa Gavrielov for my cover design and Abigail Huller for my author photo, thank you for your creativity and patience.

To Terri Boekhoff and Shirley Sinkewitsch, thank you for your professional help and friendship.

To my four-legged friends, Roxy, Bandit and Shadow, thank you for your love and kisses.

To God and all my angels who have been with me in hardship and in glory, thank you for giving me inspiration, guidance, hope, love and a shoulder to lean on.

Introduction

Suburban New York in the early seventies was a safe place to live and a great place to grow up. Crime was low. Houses were unlocked. Kids were everywhere. My parents, Tommy and Vita, had scrimped and saved so they could move us from an apartment in the Bronx to a house in the suburbs, complete with a lawn and a swing set. My only concerns were parking the Barbie Camper, wiping the dinner dishes and claiming the dog in Monopoly before my elder sister Angela or my younger sister Martha.

After I got my degree in business administration, my career ran as if it were on a time table. A year of business-to-business computer sales led to a job in the publishing industry selling advertising for computer trade magazines. Sales led to management and management led to executive positions in the high paced and lucrative world of high-tech. I followed a simple mantra: work hard, make money, work harder, get promoted, make more money. My life was like a perfectly organized slide show and I was advancing the frames as fast as I could—as if there were a grand prize for finishing early. Everything went so smoothly. I thought I was in control of my own destiny.

Suddenly, in 1984, I found myself in the middle of a storm that would engulf my family for more than a decade. It hit hard, without warning. First, my mother became ill and had to be hospitalized indefinitely. Then my sister Martha committed suicide. Then my father got cancer. Then his sister, my Aunt Yolanda, to whom I'd grown very close, was diagnosed with cancer. Between 1990 and 1994, all of them died.

I felt like I was alone in a small boat on a large ocean, facing relentless waves that pounded me again and again. At times, my career was my protective vessel, steering me away from the erratic emotional tide. At other times, there was no light in sight and I was forced to dig deep inside my soul and ask for God's help.

Eventually, I stopped resisting what was happening and concentrated my efforts on making things as good as they could be under the circumstances. I learned to embrace the storm. I learned to live inside of it and taste its salty water. I learned that under its violent surface were brilliant colors, warmth and peace. All storms end when they're good and ready. Until then, you have to grit your teeth and bail. A sense of humor helps, too. I was blessed to be born into a family that had no problem finding the funny side of pain.

This storm which devastated my family taught me that no place, person or any amount of money can shelter us from life's hardships. As human beings we're meant to experience the lows along with the highs. There is more to life than getting ahead. I learned to stop trying to advance the slides so fast. I learned to just savor the moment.

In the years following Vita's death in 1994, my career continued to flourish. My biggest promotion came in 1997, when I was asked to launch a new publication as publishing director. The project was the most challenging in my corporate career and required an almost 24/7 commitment. A year and a half after the launch, ongoing corporate power shifts continued to present challenges and opportunities.

For the first time in my life, I got attached to the job, the power, the money and the outcome. I didn't have my family problems as a point of reference anymore and I allowed my job to define who I was. The death I experienced this time was not that of a family member, but of my spirit. My health started to suffer, my energy waned, and I could feel the light of my soul getting dimmer and dimmer.

It was time to make a change, the most difficult decision in my life. I had to release the material attachments that now constituted my reality, along with all the security they provided, in order to reconnect with my spirit. In 1998, I finally decided to get off the corporate treadmill. It had served its purpose and now I needed to find mine.

I had no idea what I was going to do, nor did I care. For the first time in my life, I stood still. I stopped thinking about what was *next* and started thinking about what was *now*. I rediscovered my family, my home, my friends, my community and myself.

I realized how lucky I was to have so much love in my life, particularly from my husband Joe. He was the person who had walked beside me throughout all those years of hardship, while continuing to love me unconditionally. He was the person who taught me how powerful it was to just *be*, to not worry about the future, to live in the present.

The end of my corporate career was the beginning of a spiritual journey that has confirmed what I always believed: we are spiritual beings, connected to one another and to God. Our souls never die. We're surrounded by angels and there will always be an abundance of love to give and receive.

It was during this time of soul-searching that I decided to tell my story. I can just hear Vita saying, "I had to get sick so you could have good material for your book!" And in a way she's right. Not so much because she got sick but because she faced her illness with typical fearlessness, what I call Vita's will.

What started out to be a book about death became a book about life. Reliving my experiences through writing about them, I discovered a series of real life lessons that I can share with you. So here they are along with my story. I hope they will give you a new perspective on life and help you in your own life struggles.

I

VITA

The End

Vita, my mother, was the last to go—after my father Tommy, my Aunt Yolanda, my sister Martha. There were fewer people at her service; she was the one who had suffered the longest. The guests ushered themselves in and out quickly and quietly this time. There was nothing left to say. This death was expected and the other deaths had created a sort of numbness, making this funeral seem like an almost ordinary weekend event. When they went home, our friends would pick up where they left off an hour earlier. Some of them, though, might reflect for a moment about the unfortunate events that had plagued the Gisonni family over the past decade.

When my sister Angela and I returned to our old home that night, I suddenly noticed how weathered it looked, as if it had been suffocating in all the misery of its inhabitants. The front door, once the crisp red of an Elizabeth Arden salon door, now had a surface of cracked, dulled paint. The blue shingles were a washed-out gray with streaks of faded color that looked like frozen tears on its face. The neglected lawn was bare and brown, thirsty for new life.

The inside of the house was more like a hospital with traces of home furniture and paintings sprinkled throughout. It was exactly how Vita had left it two months earlier when she was taken to the hospital, as if she expected to be right back. Her wheelchair stood waiting for its owner directly in front of the TV, with the seat cushion still on it. I could picture her sitting there and saying in her broken English, "Oh, my ass is a-killin' me."

The surface of the marble kitchen table was barely visible under a blanket of plastic bottles of every imaginable size and color, containing enough medication for an entire hospital floor. Medical supplies filled every open shelf and surface. There were countless packages of cotton and gauze, plastic tubing, equipment, ointments, lotions, syringes, inhalants and suctioning kits.

Vita would have surely lamented the money wasted on this stuff, never to be put to use. She never wasted anything. She used to kiss stale bread before throwing it away. If she had any inkling that she was not returning, I'm positive she would have created a black market for the hospital supplies. She had always found a way to make money to support the family.

That night my sister and I lay in our childhood twin beds in our old bedroom. We looked around at the lime green walls and orange shag carpets and decided the '70s were unequivocally the worst decade for style. Angela and I were the only ones left; we were stranded on our own island, separated from the family that had once surrounded us. Our ordeal created a special bond between us. Thank God we had each other.

The eerie silence that permeated the house was comforting and haunting at the same time. It reminded me of the first night I spent in this house when I was seven years old. I couldn't sleep because I was afraid of the silence. I was accustomed to the noises of the city: the wailing sirens, the cars, the horns, the people of the night moving about talking and laughing. Later, this quiet would be replaced by the sounds of nurses coming and going, doors opening and closing, and the continuous hum of medical equipment.

Now, the silence had returned. It was finally over, as if a storm had cleared. The air was still heavy with overwhelming memories that weighed upon us, playing tricks on our eyes and ears. Pictures of the dead that surrounded us suddenly came to life, and common household noises were suddenly suspect. Our imaginations transported us into an *Abbott and Costello Meet the Monster* movie. We closed Vita's bedroom door for fear of catching a glimpse of her lying in that hospital bed, breathing laboriously, with her feet sticking out the bottom of the sheets.

We talked for hours after turning in, just as we had when we were children; neither of us wanted to give in to the night. We finally succumbed as our eyes, heavy with exhaustion, could no longer resist the sleep that beckoned us. We kept all the lights on that night. We couldn't bear the darkness.

Picture This—Sicily 1942

On the popular TV show *Golden Girls,* the character Ma, played by Estelle Getty, used to say "Picture this—Sicily, 1934" and launch into a story about her childhood. Vita got a kick out of it because those stories were close to her own memories of growing up in Sicily. The TV Ma, with her diminutive stature, zest for life, strong opinions and critical eye wasn't just make-believe. That character was my mother.

Born in 1934, Vita grew up in Sicily during World War II. Living through a war in her own backyard strengthened her survival instincts, determination and courage. Her memories of that time were not of death, suffering and hatred, but adventure and fun. Death was just a part of everyday life along with bomb shelters, grenades and German soldiers. The German tanks that occupied her town were not seen as killing machines. Her brother would sneak out late at night and play on them with the soldiers.

She often told us the story of the three sisters who died after pulling the ring off a grenade. This was to teach us how quickly life can be lost. If we ever saw a grenade lying around the streets of New York, we would know enough not to pull that ring!

After the war ended, her entire family boarded a boat to New York. She was thirteen, with two brothers and a sister. Although they had grown up on an island, none of them could swim, which made the ocean voyage quite traumatic. Vita's sister, my Aunt Mary, still cringes when she recalls the torturous two-week journey to America. Passengers, sick from the overpowering waves that continuously rocked the boat, were sprawled out on the wooden floor, unwilling and unable to stand up while the crew distributed food.

Vita means "life" in Italian. Just under five feet and weighing ninety-nine pounds, my mother was a firecracker. She lived up to her name with a feisty, energetic personality and a love of life, food and laughter. She also had a Sicilian temper. Her high cheekbones, almond-shaped hazel eyes, prominent nose and full lips were beautiful. She usually dyed her hair some shade of red, her favorite color, although she thought nothing of changing it from brown to bleached blond overnight.

Vita didn't know a word of English when she came to America, but still managed to complete a year of school in Brooklyn. She dropped out of school after eighth grade to help support the family, working as a seamstress. She did piecework, the garment industry's version of the assembly line, repeatedly sewing the same piece, such as a collar, onto garments all day long. The money she earned was directly related to her precision and speed. Her fingers moved like a machine, making her a superb worker.

She met Tommy at the factory. He was a garment cutter by day and an aspiring actor/singer by night. He had a happy-go-lucky personality, whistling while he worked, and jet-black wavy hair and dark eyes. He was also Italian and would speak to her in her native tongue. She was only sixteen; he was twenty-five. They married right before her twentieth birthday and moved to his parents' three-flat brownstone in the Bronx.

Family disputes, financial struggles and clashing personalities created a tumultuous relationship that would last all their lives. Vita was an extroverted social bug who needed a constant connection to people in and out of her family. Tommy was a loner who was most comfortable in the company of his wife and family.

They raised us with a firm hand, or in Vita's case, a shoe or wooden spoon would do. We were polite, well-groomed and quiet. We never asked for so much as a glass of water at someone else's house, nor did we ever accept one without the official nod from Vita. By today's standards, my parents would probably be considered overly protective and strict.

Vita and Tommy had mellowed as parents by the time their third daughter came along, and did not raise Martha with the same intense discipline they used on Angela and me. And since we were old enough to help, they spent less time on her care and allowed her more freedom. Martha was hardly ever spanked and when she was about to be hit would scream as if she were being tortured before they even laid a hand on her! That sort of behavior from Angela or me would have made the spanking worse but Martha managed to get off scot free.

Our birth order and individual personalities gave my sisters and I our own version of a mother-daughter love-hate relationship with Vita. Because she saw a lot of herself in me and I understood what made her tick, I had it easier than my sisters. When it came to getting what I wanted, I could play the game better. "My Debbie" was what Vita called me when talking to others, as if I were an extension of her like "my arm." Angela and Martha frequently employed me as their negotiator, to build a case for what they wanted.

Somewhere along the line I emerged as the family leader. Not in the sense of the role my mother or father played, but in terms of emotions. I was the one who pulled the family together, smoothed out the wrinkles, came up with solutions. I was also the one who made everything look doable and setbacks seem brighter. As the middle child, I welcomed this responsibility; it gave me a chance to stand out and be noticed.

Angela, the eldest, was the dutiful daughter until her teenage years, when she started pushing Vita's buttons in a constant power struggle. I was a precocious child with a feisty personality who never shut up or sat still. In my early teens I became the voice of reason. Martha, the baby, was a quiet child, but also the most stubborn, and had an awful temper.

Chores were an integral part of our daily lives. We made our beds minutes after waking up and we cleared, washed and dried the dinner dishes every evening. In August, we spent two weeks helping Vita boil and bottle bushels of fresh tomatoes to be used for sauce during the year. Vita would give us the food out of her mouth or the clothes off her back, but there would be hell to pay if we ever disrespected her. She was never satisfied with anything less than perfection.

She needed little sleep, going to bed at two in the morning and rising at five. A cigarette in one hand and black coffee in the other, I think she was the first one to claim she never inhaled. She was on the move at all times, working, doing household chores and cooking.

To her friends, Vita was the life of the party, an excellent cook and entertainer, and a dependable friend. To the kids, she was the Pied Piper. She loved children and would babysit up to six kids at a time for working mothers. This early version of daycare had an Italian twist: the kids feasted on homemade lasagna and veal parmigiana. The extra income from this helped keep the family afloat during plenty of lean years, when Tommy was out of work. On one or two occasions, we even used food stamps, although Vita was so embarrassed about this, she'd drive for miles to find a food store where no one would recognize her.

Why do bad things happen to good people? There are many theories about this. Some believe we reincarnate over and over to pay for bad karma created in past lives. We often joked with Vita about the sins she must have committed in her past lives to have suffered as much as she did in this one.

Real Life Lesson: Who you are, where you've been and what you've done all play a part in what lies ahead.

Self-Diagnosis

One midnight in the spring of 1984, Vita and I were the only ones still up. The house was quiet except for the voices on TV in the background, while Vita assembled packages. She had been doing this work at home for the last five years because it allowed her to continue babysitting during the day. Evening was her most productive time.

The table in front of her was covered with girls' play cosmetics, such as lipstick and nail polish. Vita inserted these into colorful pink retail boxes, which went into cardboard shipping boxes. Her boss picked them up once a week. She was paid a few dollars for each box and, up until now, Vita was one of the top producers. The agility she had developed in her hands as a seamstress years earlier paid off well.

That night, her fingers didn't move as fast as usual, and her headache muddied her mental sharpness. The usual spark in her eyes was gone. She normally worked until two in the morning, but tonight, like many other nights in the last few months, an unbearable headache forced her to quit early. She was taking a myriad of prescription drugs by then, but none of them seemed to work. She looked despondent, knowing that for the first time in her life something out of her control was impeding her ability to earn money.

As I said goodnight to her, she looked up at me and said, "Maybe I have a tumor in my brain."

I was tired of hearing about the headaches day in and day out. I wanted to scream, "Enough already!" But Vita still demanded respect from her children and even though I was 22, she wouldn't think twice about pulling off her shoe to whack me a good one.

So I did what I had always done as the middle child: I smoothed it over and reassured her by saying, "Ma, it's definitely not a tumor. A friend of my friend's mother has a brain tumor and that woman is barely alive. You wouldn't be able to stand up if you had a tumor."

Of course I didn't think it was a tumor. Tumors happened to other people. People I didn't know. And besides, Vita could create a melodrama out of something as trivial as a paper cut. It's a special gift that all Italian mothers have. It goes along with the need to complain regularly about their many ailments. If someone were to ask Vita how she was doing, instead of replying, "Fine," like most people, the first word out of her mouth would be "Lousy" and then she would proceed to tell them why. Usually, minor problems were portrayed as major health catastrophes.

I remember the time she told us she couldn't take two steps without extreme pain in one of her knees. Minutes later, when Angela did something that enraged her, Vita ran up the stairs to hit her!

Leave it to me, Miss Know-it-all, to say, "Ma, I thought your knee was hurting you."

She furiously replied, *"Disgraziata!"* which roughly translates to "Ungrateful child!" This expression was usually followed by a smack to the back of the head. Of course, years later when spanking fell out of public favor, Vita, using her selective memory, denied ever having laid a hand on us.

Tommy's recollection years later was that he never hit us hard. And he didn't. But he kept a battered old brown leather belt in full view at all times, as a reminder to us. It hung on a door knob. While Vita never used it on us, she was quick to remind us that Tommy would. "Wait until your father comes home" was not the kind of thing we wanted to hear!

Given the behavior pattern Vita had established while we were growing up and the fact that I didn't believe something so horrible could happen to us, I dismissed the idea of a brain tumor. Almost. No one had yet pinpointed the cause of her headaches, and they had gotten progressively worse. Since she had now started to lose her balance and choke on food, I suggested a CAT scan to her doctor the following week. I wanted to prove her wrong, but I was also afraid she might be right.

And she was. Suddenly, we became the other people that bad things happen to. It was like a slap in the face to learn misfortune didn't stop at some invisible boundary we imagined outside our doorstep. It came in without warning or invitation like that sci-fi monster, the Blob, seeping through the cracks while we weren't looking. Surprise! One day Vita is the life of the party dancing to "Mambo Italiano" and the next day she's fighting for her life.

Real Life Lesson: Listen to people with your heart instead of your ears and you will hear the truth.

I Begin to Pray

"I can't believe she has a brain tumor," I said to my sister Martha, on the plane to a two-week tour of Italy.

We'd just found out the night before that Vita had correctly guessed the source of her headaches. This, after having seen a multitude of doctors, each with a different diagnosis. The gynecologist had thought she was premenopausal. The chiropractor attributed her symptoms to a back problem. The allergist concluded allergies. At one point, her swallowing problem was diagnosed as a "floating esophagus"—whatever that is.

Our family practitioner, who had known her for years, thought she was just being her usual melodramatic, hypochondriac, dying-Italian-mother self. He finally agreed to my request for a CAT scan and, lo and behold, a large mass attached to the base of her brain was discovered.

When we heard the news, Martha and I wanted to cancel our trip to Italy, but Vita insisted we go.

She said, "Don't worry about me. I'm not gonna die yet."

We figured if she could make us take the trip and feel guilty about it, she must not be that sick. The operation wasn't scheduled until after we returned in May, and the doctors were quite optimistic, assuring us that the tumor was operable. She was expected to have a six-week recovery period in the hospital.

We arrived in Milan, went to Florence, and continued on to Rome. Then we toured the ruins of Pompeii, Capri, Naples and finally, in Sicily, we visited Vita's hometown. Like many Italian immigrants, she never went back after she left with her entire family thirty-seven years before.

The hectic pace of the trip kept us going from dawn until midnight as there was a lot to see in a short period of time. Our only relaxation was on the bus. Martha and I sat together but she didn't say much about Vita, and I didn't either.

Although Martha was a high school senior by then, she was still considered the baby of the family and we all felt protective of her. Vita encouraged us to take care of her and Martha grew up in her big sisters' shadows. She used to emulate us in the way we dressed, looked and acted.

Just about everything we bought in Italy was for Vita, as if the gifts would somehow compensate for the bad news. Maybe a cameo from Naples, rosary beads from the Vatican or a hand-embroidered linen tablecloth from Calabria would make it all go away. It was a helpless feeling, knowing that no amount of money could buy her a clean bill of health. Our only hope was to put ourselves in the hands of the doctors and have faith in God.

I worried about how Dad would deal with the whole situation. Tommy had always been the master of the house, commanding his four women to cater to his needs. Now, he was going to have to cater to Vita for a while. I didn't know if this role reversal would bring out his light-hearted, caring side, or his explosive, angry side.

The free-spirited people and culture of Italy were a welcome change from the rigid structure of American life and the news we'd left behind. There were no rules except the ones that were made to be broken, especially on the roads. Drivers zigzagged their matchbook size cars around the narrow streets using the sidewalks if necessary, while angry pedestrians shouted obscenities at them.

Our Italian bus driver was no exception. He maneuvered through the winding mountain roads of Capri as if he were Mario Andretti in the Grand Prix. I tried not to look out my window but the jagged edges of the treacherous cliffs were stunning. Far below, the crystal-clear turquoise ocean kissed the rugged terrain with gentle, intoxicating waves.

As the bus tilted and swerved around each hairpin turn, the notable absence of guardrails got me thinking about the fragility of human life. One slight, inadvertent twist of the steering wheel would send us tumbling down the cliffs to our death. One slight, inadvertent twist of the surgeon's knife would have a similar result for my mother. From this point on, the history of our family would be divided into two major periods of time—before Vita's operation and after.

I prayed a lot during that trip, although I've never considered myself a particularly religious person. Vita and Tommy made us go to mass every week until we were eighteen. After that, I chose to abandon many of the archaic rules and beliefs of the Catholic Church, although I never stopped believing in God. I believed that something or someone existed out there in the universe that stood for unconditional love, goodness and truth, which exemplified how we should live our lives. I happened to call it "God" because of my Catholic roots, but I knew He, She or It would answer to many names from other religions and cultures.

I had said the same prayers in the same order each night since I was a child. I started with the sign of the cross, the Lord's Prayer and a Hail Mary. Then I would ask for forgiveness for my sins, happiness for my family, blessings for everyone I knew (even my enemies), prayers for my deceased relatives and thanks for everything S/he's done for me. I would end with, "God, I love you." Sometimes, I would continue to ask for help with whatever was going on in my life. In Italy, I started a new addendum to my prayers. For Vita.

Dear God, please let my mother be okay after this operation. I pray to you to help the surgeon do a good job and remove all of the tumor without any problems. Thank you for finally letting us find out about this in time. I pray for her recovery. I'm sorry we didn't believe she was sick over the last two years.

Real Life Lesson: At any moment, your life can be changed forever.

Mad Science

The last normal moments in Vita's life took place the night before her operation. Dad, Angela, Martha and I were with her in her hospital room. She was very upset about having the back of her head shaved for surgery, but we quickly made her smile by telling her she'd look great as a punk rocker.

My offering was a home-cooked meal of eggplant parmigiana. I prepared the eggplant just as I had seen her do it many times before. Peeled and thinly sliced with a light coating of egg and breadcrumbs, the eggplant was sautéed and then covered with her homemade "gravy" (the name Italian-American New Yorkers give to tomato sauce) and freshly grated mozzarella cheese. When she unwrapped it, the aroma of an Italian kitchen filled the room. She had difficulty swallowing but managed to eat half. Dad polished off the rest. We joked that if this was to be her last meal, thank God it wasn't hospital food.

That night we drove forty miles to our home in Rockland County in silence, but the sound of our thoughts was deafening. Despite the city lights, it was a dark night. The taillights from the New York City daily commuters were long gone. Dad maneuvered around the ongoing construction on FDR Drive and our bodies swayed as the tires bounced over the many potholes and road patches. To our left, we heard an occasional horn echoing from the distant streets of Manhattan. To our right, we could see the lights of our hometown Bronx reflecting off the black, glassy water of the East River.

The Bronx was where I'd first encountered death. I remembered the teenage drug addict who had been killed instantly when he was pushed off the building next door, landing on the cement of our postage-stamp back yard. I remembered the man who was shot on the street in broad daylight, as Vita shoved us into the closest store for shelter. Neither of these people meant anything to me but for some reason I thought of them that night and I thought how horrible it would be if Vita died. When we got home, I realized that it was the first time since Vita gave birth to Martha that she had been away from home without us.

The most dreadful memory Vita would have about the next morning was the setup for the operation. Throughout the surgery she was to remain in an upright position with her head immobilized, her skull held in place by curved metal straps attached by rods and screws. When Vita saw this contraption, she said she felt like the main attraction in a Frankenstein movie!

The operation, lasting more than six hours, removed ninety percent of the tumor, which was benign. The remaining ten percent was wrapped around the base of the spinal cord, making it too risky to extract. By the doctors' definition, the operation was a success—in other words, the patient had survived.

Dad was there when they wheeled her out of recovery.

"Wake up, Vita! It's over," he said.

He walked alongside the gurney through the hospital corridors with the grace of a dancer. Although he was only five feet, seven inches, and forty pounds overweight, he was light on his feet.

"Wake up, Vita!" he exclaimed again in a deep, theatrical voice.

Slowly she opened her eyes. He then noticed the tube protruding from her neck, connected to a respirator. Apparently, they had performed a tracheotomy during the operation to help her breathe.

When the nurses brought her into the intensive care unit, they asked her to move her arms and legs. She couldn't. The doctors said her body was in a state of shock from the surgery and most functions would return to normal in a few days. She seemed frustrated and pained but couldn't speak. Dad quickly suggested she use her eyes: two blinks for "yes" and one blink for "no."

Within days, she was able to move her hands and feet, but other abilities didn't return. Her breathing became erratic whenever they tried to lessen her dependency on the respirator. She couldn't coordinate her body movements to walk, stand or even sit up in bed. Since her gag reflex (which prevents food from entering the lungs during swallowing) was not functioning, she couldn't eat. So another opening was cut into her stomach and a gastrostomy, or feeding tube, inserted. A urinary catheter was the third device connected to her body, completing her new look.

The two sections of the brain that the tumor had rested on were the cerebellum, which coordinates body movement, and the brain stem, which is responsible for basic life functions such as breathing and swallowing. Before the surgery, she had moderate difficulty in these areas. After surgery, her condition was worse. In our opinion, the operation was not a success.

The weeks after surgery became an eye-opening introduction to hospital life. On one of my regular visits to the hospital, I was told that Vita was in therapy. She could be taken off the respirator by then for short periods of time. The rehabilitation unit was a large room filled with disabled patients, therapists and all sorts of exercise equipment. It looked like a gym for the Special Olympics.

I immediately saw Vita at the back of the room. It was the first time I had seen her in a standing position in the three weeks since the operation. Around her wrists, ankles and waist were leather straps that held her in place up against a giant wheel.

As soon as I got close to her she said, "Debbie, get a gun and starta shoot me. I justa need the balloons."

We both started laughing. She really did look like part of a circus act. I found out later that day that the wheel was supposed to help her get her sense of balance back, so she could stand on her own. She stayed on it for fifteen minutes each day.

Another interesting piece of equipment was the special lift that the nurses used to move Vita from her hospital bed to a wheelchair and back. Two nurses could have easily picked up her slight 100-pound frame but instead, they opted for a mechanical apparatus to hoist her in and out. It was supposed to be safer for the patient and easier on the nurses' backs, but one look at it had me thinking otherwise.

A miniature crane which hoisted a cloth seat, this device needed to operate at a height that seemed dangerously high. Getting Vita situated in the exact position necessary was itself a huge production. She was so small that she kept flopping over on the seat with a look of terror on her face, hoping she wouldn't fall out. She looked like a boulder being moved around by a construction crew. After a while, the nurses went back to the old-fashioned method of picking her up.

Whenever we saw another strange medical contraption, we'd get the same puzzled look, with our heads cocked to one side just like a dog watching a vacuum cleaner for the first time.

Although Vita had been in the hospital for a month, I felt optimistic she would recover soon.

Dear God, Thank you for Vita's life and her having survived the operation, but it's been over a month and she's suffered so much. Please help her get better. She looks so sad and frustrated. She wants to get better. Give her the strength she needs. You've always answered my prayers. I know you'll answer this one. She has to be able to walk again and eat again or she'll just die. This wasn't supposed to happen. She was supposed to be home by now.

Should I have prayed harder for her or done something else? Are you punishing her for crying wolf all those years or punishing us for not listening? Maybe if I had asked the doctor for a CAT scan earlier, the tumor wouldn't have grown so big. But how was I to know? Why didn't we all pay more attention?

Real Life Lesson: No matter how many machines modern medicine invents, it's the personal connection that heals people.

The Alphabet

Many people who stay hooked up to respirators for months are incoherent, unconscious or both. Vita was neither. Due to the position of the tumor, her breathing capacity was the first to suffer when her condition fluctuated. She remained an alert, vivacious woman who loved to talk. The respirator tube that connected to her tracheotomy opening blocked her vocal cords, making it impossible for her to speak. So the life-sustaining respirator was also a source of great frustration.

For the first couple of days after the operation, the eye blink code of "yes" and "no" worked fine. After the first week, however, the lack of more in-depth communication started to get to her. When she became agitated, her erratic breathing set off a warning beep on the respirator, alerting the nurses to increase the output. This no doubt prolonged her reliance on the dread machine.

The hospital's physical therapists suggested using a small plastic alphabet board. The idea was for her to point to letters in order to spell out words and even sentences. Vita, desperate to communicate, was eager to try. There were just a few more obstacles to perfect communication.

The operation had left her with little control of her dominant right side. She was forced to use her left hand to point to the letters, which was difficult for her.

There was another problem. Vita's version of English combined Italian roots with Brooklynese, laced with her own private expressions. Like many Italians, Vita had trouble pronouncing words that ended with a consonant. Sometimes she would just add a vowel, such as saying *spasma* for *spasm*. That was easy to understand. Other times, however, she would completely change a word. To her, a good piece of cake was not *moist*, it was *moistra*. Instead of soy sauce, she sprinkled *sui sauce* on her Chinese food.

Words that did not roll off her tongue easily were replaced by similar words. Unfortunately, the replacement word already had an entirely different meaning. So when our dog Junior couldn't see well anymore, Vita said she had *Cadillacs,* instead of *cataracts*. When I used to exercise on a mini trampoline that I kept at the house, she would say I was doing my *robots* instead of *aerobics*. American idioms were always tough for Vita. She once told someone that she'd quit smoking *cold duck*.

Those well-meaning physical therapists never guessed that using the alphabet board with my mother would be like playing a cross between Wheel of Fortune and Password. We were forever trying to find the missing letter or the hidden meaning. The family was much better at it than the nurses, since we were familiar with Vita's manner of speaking before the operation, but sometimes she even had us stumped. We could spend fifteen minutes on one word and still not get it. Then Vita, the "game show host," would decide if the word was worth pursuing, which was usually a matter of how many warning beeps she got from the respirator as she anxiously tried to mouth the words.

As frustrating as it was for both her and us, this little game was a lot of fun to play. When we got it right, it was as if we had hit the jackpot. We would clap, jump up and down, and high-five each other. On the surface it looked like a silly game but underneath, it was much more. This hilarious mix of mismatched words and feelings was a much-needed break from the uncertainty of her physical condition.

As a family, we weren't like TV's Bradys or Cleavers, who encouraged each other to express personal feelings. The atmosphere in our house was a cross between the high drama and explosive energy of the Bunkers in *All in the Family* and the middle class, '60s suburban mentality of the Arnolds in *The Wonder Years*. We needed props to demonstrate our love. For many years to come, each time Vita landed back on a respirator, the alphabet game reconnected her to the family circle, which she desperately needed. Playing the game reconnected us with our unconditional love for her.

Real Life Lesson: Sometimes, the most important message to communicate is your commitment to communicate.

Village Life

The intensive care unit, or ICU, in the hospital was one large room with twelve patients' beds positioned along three walls. On the fourth wall was the nurses' station. The light walls, gleaming linoleum floors and blur of doctors' white coats coming and going made the atmosphere sterile and bright. Most of the patients were connected to intravenous lines that slowly dripped life-saving liquid into their veins.

Above each bed was a U-shaped metal track and a cloth curtain. These curtains, which could be pulled around the bed to enclose the patient for private consultations or procedures, were seldom used in ICU. The patients were too ill to care about someone else catching a glimpse of a private part or learning their business.

The constant noise level from humans and machines, and the endless flurry of activity in and out, made me wonder how anyone got any sleep. Patients were continually being transferred via gurneys from the ICU to other departments, such as x-ray or radiation, with their medical paraphernalia trailing behind them. Conversations and movement among doctors, nurses, patients and visitors were visible and audible to anyone in the room. It was like watching a soap opera with a dozen mini stories all happening at once.

One day, while Vita was in the ICU, a battered old man was admitted. He was followed by five men in dark suits. Our curiosity was immediately piqued, as the men were not your typical ICU visitors, particularly once they started questioning the man in a low whisper. "Who did this to you? Did you recognize them? How many were there?" It was like a scene from *The Godfather*. Guards posted at the door asked every visitor to state their name and who they were visiting. When we left for lunch, we saw news vans, cameras and press people hovering outside the hospital.

As sick as she was, Vita was intrigued by the new arrival and kept her eyes and ears open. She was able to find out the who, what, where, when and how within an hour! By the time we returned, she told us that the man, who had been beaten and robbed, was the father-in-law of a highly visible political figure in New York. The "suits" were trying to determine if this was a random act of violence or a personal threat, due to his son-in-law's policies. The whole incident created a buzz throughout the hospital, particularly in the ICU where the man remained for several days.

Media attention was not the norm for the average hospital patient, but that didn't make their stories any less important. They each had a story and Vita wanted to know it. She actually preferred the ICU to the regular hospital unit: the service was better and there was more going on to keep her mind off the pain. Her participation in the hospital drama, even if only as a spectator, kept her going. She knew the names, backgrounds, secrets and ambitions of everyone who walked through that ICU door. As one of the many characters of hospital life, Vita felt perfectly comfortable among these strangers who would otherwise never have crossed her path. Their common suffering brought them together, equalizing the playing field and connecting them as human beings. Famous or ordinary, rich or poor, they all bled the same.

Vita could have easily chosen to isolate herself in her own misery and drown in a sea of pain, self-pity and loneliness. Instead, she shared her passion for life with the strangers who lived and worked inside the hospital walls. She commiserated with the person in the adjacent bed, gave advice to the nurse with boyfriend problems and compared cultural rituals with the Jamaican doctor. She took the time to get to know people and their families. When we visited her, she would bring us into her new world by telling us the stories behind the curtains and the white coats. Before we knew it, we were part of the drama ourselves, intrinsically linked to a story much larger than our own, a story about the lives of many.

Real Life Lesson: Your connection to others, inside and outside the family, gives your life its meaning.

Visiting Hours

After six weeks in the hospital, Vita was transferred to a chronic care hospital and nursing home in Rockland County. She stayed there for the next two and a half years, followed by six months in a rehabilitation facility. The doctors who had originally estimated a maximum hospital stay of six weeks gave us no hope that she would ever come home again. During a thousand plus consecutive nights away from home, her only connection to her family and friends was during visiting hours.

When I visited, I would sometimes stop outside her doorway to watch her. She would be staring up at the ceiling, looking as if the life had been sucked out of her—until the moment she saw me. Then her eyes would light up and a smile would emerge on her face, transforming her into another person. I loved the fact that she loved to see me and that I could have such a positive effect on her, just by being there.

After the hello kisses, she would get right down to hospital business and tell me what she wanted me to do: flip her pillow, place a cold compress on her forehead, change her gown or refill the ice water. When she was able to sit in a wheelchair, she'd ask me to wheel her around the hospital for a change of scenery.

For the first three years after her operation, Vita needed intense hospital care. There was nothing I could do to change the fact that she had to stay in the hospital. What I could do, however, was make her stay more palatable. I got large, colorful posters from computer vendors at the trade shows I attended. They were essentially promotional pieces for companies like Apple, Hewlett Packard or IBM. Vita didn't know anything about these companies' products and in most cases, didn't understand the message on the poster. That didn't matter. They made her feel good. They put some color on the bland white hospital walls. They gave her something to focus on and look at. They gave her something to talk about: "My daughter sent these to me from a computer trade show in Las Vegas." They reminded her of me!

I also sent her cards at least two times a week that she could display in her room. I chose the biggest ones I could find and added all sorts of colorful stickers to the inside. I knew she couldn't read well after her operation, so I focused on the pictures and used thick magic markers to write messages.

Angela crocheted a big bright red blanket for her room. This had the same effect as my posters, plus Vita could brag about her daughter's domestic capabilities!

On several occasions, I sneaked our family dog Junior in under my coat for a visit. Junior was a terrier-poodle-cocker mutt with curly black hair who weighed only fifteen pounds. Junior was a *she*. We had relied upon the expert opinion of our family friend Pat Foyder, a nurse, who thought *she* was a *he* until after we'd named her. Junior brought some excitement to the visit as I circumvented guard stations, nurses' desks and staff before reaching Vita's room on the third floor. Junior, a very high-strung and yappy dog, remained unusually quiet during the entire visit. She allowed Vita to pet her and responded with wet, loving kisses. She sensed that Vita was sick and stayed on her best behavior.

The family saw Vita almost every day, but our jobs and responsibilities could not be put on hold indefinitely. We managed to spend an hour or two with her a few nights during the week and more time on the weekends. After months of this schedule, boredom set in. Once we'd caught up with the news both in and out of the hospital, talked about her progress, did what she asked us to do, and watched some TV, there was little to do but sit on hard chairs for hours. I brought friends with me whenever I could, to help stretch the conversation and pass the time.

My social life during that time became virtually non-existent, replaced by household duties and hospital visits. Thank God, I had already met Joe, my soul mate. The moment Joe and I met we were viscerally attracted to each other, as if we had known and loved each other for a thousand years. Joe was kind and gentle with an upbeat, easy-going personality and a great sense of humor. Women drooled over his piercing blue eyes and radiant smile but he never seemed to notice. He remained completely humble about his looks.

Best friends and lovers, we knew not everyone has the pleasure of this sort of bond. Joe ended up becoming part of my family. He would talk more with my sisters than with his own siblings. Throughout Vita's troubles, he was right there, every moment. He was just as comfortable accepting a date with Vita and me at the hospital, as a date at the movies. Sometimes he would drop in on Vita by himself just to say hello. Understandably, she was quite fond of him.

Visiting may be hard duty but having to leave is even worse. I always felt selfish because I wanted to go home. I tried to rationalize my feelings by reminding myself that the situation wasn't a typical two-week hospital stay and that any normal human being would long to go home, but I knew in my heart that Vita didn't see it that way. She would've rented us a bed in the same room and moved us in if she could have.

Whenever I'd get ready to leave she would say, "You're leaving?" It was the same tone I'd heard as a teenager when she'd say, "You're wearing *that*?"

I knew exactly what she meant. She had meant, "Change your outfit" and now she meant, "Stay another hour or two." So I would stay a while longer. Finally, I learned to start leaving earlier than I really expected to be able to go.

Sometimes I would resort to an Italian daughter's only defense against Italian-mother-induced guilt. I call it *reversal of guilt*. I would say something like, "Ma, I'm getting so sleepy, and the roads are dark and icy. You wouldn't want me to get into an accident, would you?"

She would respond, "Go home, you look tired," as if it were her idea in the first place.

And then, of course, I'd really feel guilty and stay another half-hour! Vita two, Debbie one. Oh, well!

For a short while, Vita's friends came to see her on a regular basis but after the first few months their visits tapered off. Her sister Mary didn't live close enough to visit often and since she didn't drive, was dependent on others to bring her. Vita's closest friends before the operation weren't necessarily the ones who were around afterwards. In fact, she developed very close friendships with people she barely knew before she was ill.

One such person was Tommy's co-worker Van, whom Vita met after her operation. I never knew his last name and I'm not sure Van was his real first name, but it didn't matter. He started visiting Vita two or three times a week. He used to sit for hours with her, sometimes in silence. I was amazed and thankful for this person who came out of nowhere to spend time with someone he hadn't known before.

Old friends who had lost touch over the years suddenly became part of Vita's life again, like Pat Foyder, her partner in crime in the '70s. They used to go everywhere together, piling all us children into the back seats of Pat's big blue station wagon. Pat had a cheery personality offset by sarcastic wit. Hers was just the kind of attitude Vita needed and Pat was the only one she'd take it from. She was like family to us.

Rob and Michael McKiernan, whom Vita used to baby-sit years before, started coming around with their mother, Una. Maria Riverso, an old friend of the family's from the Bronx, was in her seventies and had to take two buses to get to the hospital. Mrs. Drivas and Mrs. Brophy, the mothers of two of my best friends in high school, started to come around frequently. Mrs. Drivas brought her friend Mary, who then started coming on her own, even though she hardly knew Vita.

The people who touched Vita's life when she needed it most were true angels on earth. When others had forgotten about her, they were there out of pure and simple kindness towards another human being. They gave her one of life's greatest gifts: unconditional friendship.

I saw so many lonely faces of people in long-term care facilities who looked like they had been forgotten by their family and friends. It was hard to imagine they had once had normal lives outside the hospital, but I knew they did, just like Vita. They desperately needed a connection to the outside world and craved the company of a warm body—known or unknown, young or old, human or animal.

God, thank you for all of Ma's old and new friends who come to visit her. I wish more would come. I'm so angry with some of her old friends who have stopped seeing her. Ma was always there for them. How dare they forget about her? People can't understand what we've been going through as a family. Sometimes I think that they figure as long as she's still alive, everything must be okay.

I can't bear to think about her lying alone in that hospital bed night after night. She must hate it. She must hate her life and everything she's missing. I know I would. I'm sick about all of it. How long can this go on?

Forgive me, but I sometimes think it would be better if she were a vegetable. That way, she wouldn't know how bad things really are. Everything she loved in life has been taken away from her and the doctors don't seem to care. Don't you care about her? About us? Please, let her get better. At least let her eat again.

She's suffered so much already. Why? She's a good person. Why are you doing this to her? Every time she gets better, she gets worse. How long can she take it? How long can we take it? How will we survive if she never gets out? She'll die a slow death in there while Dad dies a slow death outside. He needs her. I don't think he can take any more pain. He's letting me deal with all the doctors by myself now.

I'm sorry, but sometimes when I visit her, I think she wants our pity. I resent her wanting it, even if she does deserve it. I hate going to the hospital day after day. I hate the fact she can't do anything for herself. I look forward to seeing her, but then I can't wait to leave. She's so dependent and weak. I don't want to take care of a child. I want the old Vita back again.

Real Life Lesson: The simplest gestures of kindness can make the biggest difference in a person's life, including your own.

Life on the Outside

Vita's life was on hold while she was ill and she had no say in the matter. Being confined to a hospital was like serving a prison sentence, particularly with limited physical control of her body. Her room was her cell, and she was dependent upon those in charge to let her in and out. She lost privileges she had taken for granted, like sharing evenings at home with her family or cooking a special holiday dinner. Her daily routine was regulated by others who controlled when she could eat, bathe or receive visitors. Although there were plenty of times she wanted to scream at the top of her lungs, she opted not to—for fear of being taken away in a straight jacket!

Her priorities changed from taking care of a family and household to struggling with basic life functions such as breathing and swallowing. She had physical therapy classes to help her regain control of the large muscles in her arms and legs. Occupational therapy redeveloped fine motor skills in her hands and fingers. Respiratory therapists patted her back, as if they were burping a baby, in order to clear her lungs. Vita listened diligently to all the instructions, practicing her exercises eagerly, never giving up, but progress was slow and each time she advanced, another setback would occur.

During the first three years, she contracted pneumonia at least eight times, with each incident sending her back to the ICU on a respirator for weeks at a time. This chronic condition weakened her lungs until her regular breathing capacity was only fifty percent on a good day.

It seemed hardly fair that she was fighting for her life every day while other people were enjoying theirs. Our family was stuck in a time warp while everything around us continued.

During the years Vita was in the hospital, we received the news that three close friends had passed away. One was her friend Pat Foyder's husband John, who burned to death in a car accident. A car crash instantly killed another friend, Tina, who had been kind enough to bring Dad, Martha and me a home-cooked chicken dinner just days before.

When a childhood friend of mine died of leukemia, I realized that we were as guilty of neglecting our friends as I had accused them of being. I didn't take the time to console the families, visit them or attend funeral services. When one of my best friends, Coleen, was diagnosed with a brain tumor, I didn't reach out to her. I was too caught up in my own family's problems.

Despite having one foot inside the hospital door at all times, our lives—Dad's, Martha's, Angela's and mine—continued on the outside. To give Vita a brief glimpse of what was going on outside her world, we'd have birthday celebrations in her room, with cake, presents and singing. I'd practice a speech I was going to give in front of her, so she got a taste of what I was doing at work. We would bring manicure sets in to do her nails. On her high school graduation day, Martha visited Vita in her cap and gown.

When I was traveling for business, I would call her from hotel rooms and airports. She would always ask me where I was. She had no idea where these cities were, but thought I must be important if my company sent me there. She would brag to her visitors, "My daughter is in Boston today." It was another way I could bring the world into her hospital room and get her mind off where she was.

Dad continued to grow tired and resentful of his life without a wife and his countless trips to the hospital. Mounting medical expenses forced him to sell Vita's diamond engagement ring and convert the lower floor of our house into a rental unit. He even left his job in the garment industry for a county government service job in order to secure better health benefits.

Of all of us, I had the most dramatic changes in my life. I had been selling advertising for a small telecommunications magazine. A year after Vita's operation, I was offered a job in Northern California. The new job was a premier sales territory in Silicon Valley for a computer publication. This represented a considerable career advancement and raise.

My friends and family never thought I would move away from my mother, given her condition, to take a job in California. I was the one she was closest to and who had taken charge of the situation, organizing things and talking to doctors. The thought would never have crossed my own mind if I hadn't been approached by my company. My initial answer was No, although if things had been normal at home, I would have said Yes in a heartbeat. They gave me more time to think about it and I did.

Maybe somewhere in the back of my mind I knew that I couldn't keep up the pace of my life in New York. I was so involved in holding everything together, it was mind-boggling. I spent three to four hours a day commuting to a full-time job. Then there were Vita's health concerns (which meant dealing with doctors and insurance companies, and doing research), necessary emotional support (Vita at the hospital, Dad and Martha at home), plus running the household (cooking a big meal each night, grocery shopping, cleaning, laundry). How long could I do it? How long would I want to do it?

Actually, I didn't think about all that. I just thought what an excellent job opportunity it was that would allow me to live in a place I've always wanted to live. I didn't go through a bunch of "what if" scenarios. That wasn't how I made decisions. What-ifs were never relevant; they only served to confuse the issue. Some people thought I was running away from my troubles, but I didn't see it that way. I thought I could still be an enormous help to my family, without having to miss a great opportunity. The decision was one of the hardest in my life, but I followed my gut. It took a lot of courage.

My California office was located just fifteen minutes away from my Aunt Yolanda's house in Redwood City. Yolanda was Dad's younger sister. I had visited her twice during college breaks and fallen in love with the West Coast, thinking I might move there some day. Although the timing of the move could not have been worse, I slowly convinced myself it was the right thing for my career. Martha was now old enough to handle the household; Angela lived forty-five minutes away; and besides, there was no guarantee Vita would ever come home. The job would allow me to travel back to New York at least once a month and, with the added income, I could help support the family.

I ran the idea by Vita and Tommy. I knew in their hearts they didn't want me to leave, but I also knew the high value they placed on education and career. They never once asked that I stay and so I left. I spent six months living with my Aunt Yolanda and Uncle Joe. Then my Joe, without ever having visited California, without asking any questions, moved out to join me.

I spoke to Vita on the phone nearly every day. When I traveled back to New York I would stretch my trips out to spend time with her and help with the house, doctor's visits or whatever else she and Dad needed done.

Beyond the nucleus of our family and friends, major world events took place while Vita was sick. From the time of her operation in 1984 until her death ten years later, she would see the Challenger space shuttle explode on the TV in her hospital room, hear about the collapse of Communism in the Soviet Union and witness the fall of the Berlin Wall. Apartheid would end in South Africa, a nuclear plant explosion in Chernobyl would kill seven thousand people and a bomb on Pan Am Flight 103 would explode and scatter the remains of 270 people over Lockerbie, Scotland. Major events like these made our plight seem miniscule by comparison.

During those same years, I continued my nightly chats with God and it was S/he who heard my innermost feelings throughout this ordeal. I never cried in front of Vita and she never cried in front of me. Sadness wasn't something we were comfortable displaying. When I saw her, I kept a smile on my face and an upbeat outlook for her sake as well as mine, but at night I pleaded with God, rather than prayed.

I didn't get it. Life was good to me; it always had been. I had a wonderful partner and a skyrocketing career. I lived in one of the best places on earth, making more money than I'd ever imagined. Everything would've been perfect if it were not for Vita's situation, which seemed to spill over into every aspect of my life. It was always there in the background of my thoughts, toying with my emotions, scraping me with its sharp unpredictability. I hated it because it was the one thing in my life I couldn't control or fix.

Dear God, thank you for all that you've given me in this life, but why must my family suffer? I love them so much and it kills me that I can't make their lives as good as mine. I always thought I could.

If you can't help Ma, I'd rather you just take her and be done with it. At least it would end her pain. I'm sorry to think that but I just can't help myself. I'd rather see her dead than suffer like this.

Thank you for California. I feel it's my destiny to be here with Joe but at the same time, I feel terrible for leaving. I know a lot of people think I'm heartless and callous to leave my family in this situation. I don't know. Am I?

I don't think I could have lived like that much longer without exploding. I don't want to take care of everyone and everything anymore: Martha, Dad, the house, Vita, the doctors, the insurance companies, my own job. I can't please them all. This new job rescued me. I think I can help more if I don't live in that situation day after day.

I don't understand why things go so well for me and not for them. I'm grateful but I wish I could spread some of my luck to my family. Please help Martha and Dad get along. Please have Angela help more. Please let Vita come home soon. Bless them all.

Real Life Lesson: Having a perfect life is a myth because you can never perfect what is always changing.

She's Back!

In 1987, Vita was finally released from the hospital. The thought of her coming home filled our hearts with both joy and sadness. Knowing that she was leaving hospital life behind was exhilarating, but we had always imagined her coming home in better physical condition than when she'd left. She'd never again have one hundred percent breathing capacity, walk on her own or be self-sufficient.

Although she no longer needed a respirator, her situation required a hospital setting to be recreated at home, complete with hospital bed, standing bed tray, oxygen tank, wheelchair, nebulizer, suctioning machine and medical supplies. Even the bathroom needed to be fitted with a handicap toilet seat and railing. None of these inconveniences mattered because we were so thankful she could come home. We located a home-nursing agency that could handle her 24-hour staffing needs, with nurses changing shifts every eight hours. Thankfully, some old and new friends started visiting and helping out as well. Most of them were neighbors like Jane two houses down, Dottie across the street, or our new tenant downstairs, Janice.

Dad desperately wanted Vita home after the nightmare of the last three years but at the same time, I knew he was uncomfortable opening up his home and his life to strangers. Tommy's home represented all that was important to him: his family and his privacy. His home was his castle and he was the king. And now, with Vita's care being top priority, his status and importance as ruler of the house would fade into the background. Sharing his private domain would be challenging, but he was prepared to do it for Vita. He willingly moved his belongings into a small guest bedroom and set up the master bedroom for her.

The furniture in the rest of the house was kept exactly as it had been before Vita left. It was a combination of Mediterranean clutter with a touch of plastic. The living room had red wall-to-wall carpeting, a Spanish bullfighter painting and custom-made plastic covers on the crushed velvet couch. On a typical New York summer day with a ninety-degree temperature, ninety-percent humidity and no air conditioning, you'd have to painfully peel yourself off the couch!

During the two years Martha and Dad lived together, they'd formed a close relationship. Martha was still the baby of the family in his eyes: the one who cuddled up to him long after the age that Angela and I had stopped, which gave him a special fondness for her. Despite the circumstances, they created a relatively normal living environment that drastically changed when Vita returned. Vita re-entered their lives like a tornado: she uprooted all that had become stable and exposed everything that had been considered private to the strangers she relied upon for her care and well-being.

When Vita came home, she expected to pick up where she'd left off three years earlier, regardless of the fact that everything had changed. She expected to find her black leather purse in the same closet she had always kept it in. Ditto for the money she hid in an envelope in the linen closet, the picture of her mother on the kitchen windowsill, the bathing suit in the second drawer of her dresser or the book of matches in the desk drawer.

Like a member of the Spanish Inquisition, Vita relentlessly accused Martha and Dad of throwing away her personal possessions. They had been forced to discard many items when they rented the bottom floor of the house, but that was not an acceptable excuse to Vita, who was desperately trying to put the pieces of her old life back together again.

Despite all that had happened, Vita still wanted to live her life by the same old set of rules. These were the multitude of how-to instructions that included the one and only way things should be done, whether it was mixing pasta sauce or vacuuming the carpet. It was Vita's way. These rules were ingrained into Vita's personality, regardless of the situation, and never to be changed or improved upon.

When we were growing up, my sisters and I would joke about the invisible book of rules that existed in our mother's head that turned Saturday cleaning days into boot camp. She would dole out assignments and inspect every inch of our work, always finding the one spot we missed and making us do it over. We used to secretly call her the Warden.

Vita's intense, uncompromising personality was the glue that held the family together, and we had learned long ago not to challenge her. Now, although her body didn't work as well as before, her mind still did. That meant she was back in control of the house, all rules enforced. This wasn't easy for Martha and Tommy.

My trips back to New York became more frequent because I traveled more for my job as my responsibilities increased. I stayed at the house whenever I could. Vita's "happy to see me" face would be followed by instructions on what she needed me to do for her. Sometimes she'd ask me to go up into the attic to look for something. I always said a silent prayer first, hoping that Martha or Dad hadn't thrown away whatever it was she wanted.

During my visits, I slept in my old bedroom, right next door to Vita's. There was always a nurse in the room with her to monitor the machine that delivered a constant mist of oxygen into her tracheotomy opening. Vita couldn't speak at night because of this treatment so she would often get nervous and have a breathing seizure. The commotion would wake me up and I would stand in her doorway to watch while the nurse used what's called an "ambu bag" to blow air into Vita's lungs. If Vita was putting on a show to get my sympathy, it certainly worked. After the episode, I could never get back to sleep.

The next morning, Vita would inevitably tell me about her dreams. They were always happy dreams with her loved ones singing, eating, laughing, dancing and enjoying life without a care in the world. In her dreams, she was healthy and vibrant, and her body was free and light as a feather. It was the only place where she could escape the reality of her dreadful physical condition.

Thank you, thank you, thank you, God for finally letting her come home after all these years! Please let this be a good turning point for all of us.

I'm sorry I'm not living there, but I cannot come back. My life is in California with Joe and Aunt Yolanda. She's like a second mother to me and I feel that she needs me here.

I pray that Martha, Dad and Ma can all get along well at home with the nurses. Maybe she won't need nurses forever. I hope the nurses don't drive Dad nuts. I hope he doesn't drive them nuts.

I hope having Ma home doesn't make things worse for Dad and Martha. There's so much equipment, so many people. I'm afraid Dad will just explode if things don't run smoothly. Please give Dad patience and understanding. I know he's been through a lot but he has to rise to the occasion and give Ma support.

I hope Martha will be okay. Ma and Dad never did make the same demands on her. Things don't seem to bother her.

Real Life Lesson: Don't assume a person's physical condition is a reflection of their spirit.

**Vita at home with her girls,
Debbie, Angela and Martha (L-R)
1987**

II

MARTHA

The Phone Call

By 1990, Vita's struggle with chronic illness had been an ongoing battle for six years. Tommy was recuperating from hip replacement surgery, relying on Martha to help him get around. She was still living at home, working part-time, and going to college. Joe and I had been happily married for two years and Angela was living on her own.

One evening in April of that year, I was home watching television in Foster City, California, where Joe and I rented a condo. Feeling unusually restless and nervous, I kept telling Joe that I didn't feel right but I couldn't explain why. My skin felt like ants were crawling all over it. When the phone rang and it was Dad, I expected bad news, since he rarely called. I assumed something had happened to Vita.

His voice was trembling as he cried, "Debbie—something terrible—something terrible has happened. Your sister Martha killed herself."

I heard the words but I couldn't believe them. I thought it was a mistake. Martha would never do anything as foolish as that.

"What happened!" I screamed.

"She shot herself in her car."

My entire body started to quiver. I felt like I was shoved under water, as if water filled my lungs until the very core of my soul was being crushed by the incredible pressure.

As I hung up the phone, everything seemed to move in slow motion. When I broke the news to Joe, we were in such shock we couldn't even cry. We kept asking ourselves how she could possibly do this to herself. What had provoked her?

Somehow, I made arrangements to fly to New York the next morning. We packed and waited.

I thought about how I had felt before the phone call. Had Martha's soul swept through my body with the same violence as her death? Or was it a foreboding of the news to come?

Later that night, I spoke to Angela and learned that she had a similar experience. She went to bed around 10:30 but couldn't sleep because she was anxious and unable to breathe. She turned on the TV as a distraction but couldn't shake the feeling that something was wrong, very wrong. Then the phone rang. It was 11:30, Eastern time. She heard Vita's sobbing voice.

"Angela," she said, crying hysterically, "something happened to Martha."

A man came on the line, saying he was a state trooper. "Can you come down here? Your sister's been in an accident."

Instead of asking, "Is she okay?" Angela asked, "Is she dead?"

Somehow, she knew.

When Angela arrived at our parents' house, three police cars were parked outside; two of them belonged to state troopers. She ran up the front lawn, never feeling her legs beneath her. She spotted Dad first. He was sitting alone in his favorite chair with tears running down his face. Angela, crying herself, went up to him. He looked right through her and started talking in a low whisper to himself.

"She broke my heart," he cried. "That kid broke my heart."

He would never be the same.

Vita was in her wheelchair, crying hysterically with two nurses trying to calm her down. When she started to hyperventilate, one of the nurses gave her a portable inhalant. They wanted to call an ambulance but Vita vehemently objected. She repeatedly screamed, "No ambulance! I'm not going!"

She had lost control of her emotions. Angela ran over and slapped her across the face, in an attempt to bring her back to reality. Her screams subsided into sobs while the nurses struggled to give her a sedative.

Although Angela, Tommy and Vita were in the same room, they were emotionally disconnected. Their minds were racing in separate directions, grasping for pieces of data that might help them understand what had happened. They blamed themselves. They blamed each other. Vita and Tommy's relationship, never peaceful and recently strained by Vita's poor health, was facing another challenge: the loss of their youngest child.

I'm still haunted by Dad's heartbroken voice on the phone that night; it's like a bad song playing over and over in my head. Each time I heard it I wished I could change the words, change that terrible night and the rage inside my soul.

God, this can't be happening to us! God, please tell me this isn't true. Tell me this is all a bad dream or a mistake. I can't believe she's dead. I can't believe I will never see her again. Oh God, the pain is excruciating. I'm drowning. I can't breathe. How will we go on? Ma and Dad will never get through this. It hurts me more to think of their pain.

Martha, I hate you! If you're out there somewhere and you can hear me, I hate you for what you've done. How could you be so stupid and selfish? Didn't you know this would kill Ma and Dad? Did you want to hurt them with the ultimate temper tantrum? You always take the easy way out, don't you? But this time, we can't fix your mistake and you can't undo it! Now we're stuck with your problems.

What the fuck happened, Martha? Did someone kill you and make it look like suicide? I can't believe you'd do it. Don't think for a minute that I'm going to blame myself for this. This is your doing, not mine. Maybe you had a screw loose in your head but mine's been on straight all my life and I'm not gonna let you mess with it!

Oh, Martha you poor soul. What went wrong? Who or what pushed you over the edge?

How will we get through this? God, help us.

Real Life Lesson: Anyone in your life can be gone in an instant.

The Flaky One

By morning I was a wreck. My muscles felt like they had been pummeled and torn from my bones. I was unable to consciously move in any given direction, as if my brain were somewhere outside my body. Conflicting emotions swirled around inside me. Anger mixed quickly with fear, which was then diluted by sadness or pity or suspicion. I tried to stop the flow but all I could do was reduce it to a slow trickle, which ended up feeling like some sick water torture. The more I tried to get it out of my mind, the louder it dripped, reminding me of the terrible loss. I was not going to escape it. I was too weak to try.

Joe and I managed to get ourselves to the airport. Once there, I had hoped to find relief amidst the crowd of strangers on the plane, but the thoughts in my head only became louder. I cried during most of the flight as memories of Martha flashed through my mind.

Just two weeks earlier when I was in New York on business, she'd seemed happy and full of life. I had the pictures with me we took that weekend. She looked like any other healthy twenty-two-year-old woman, smiling, arm-in-arm with her two sisters. Beyond the family resemblance, we each had a unique look. Angela had inherited the family's light brown wavy hair and hazel eyes, while I got the black curly hair and olive skin. Martha was a combination, her long, straight black hair complementing light skin and pale gray-blue eyes. At five feet five inches, she was an inch taller than Angela and I, with a thin frame and long legs.

I remembered how excited Angela and I were when Vita brought Martha home from the hospital in 1966. I was five and Angela was eight. Martha was like a doll to play with. We couldn't wait to hold her. Although we were forbidden to do so without parental supervision, we used to sneak into the bedroom and pick her up. There was something about having a baby sister that made us want to take care of her forever.

Angela and I had always been there for Martha, to the best of our ability. When she needed help in school, we gave it to her. When she bought her first car, I gave her the down payment and Angela and I taught her how to drive. When she needed a job, I gave her the necessary contacts. She followed me in just about every part-time job I ever had, from bank teller to women's retail sales.

Although she seemed perfectly comfortable with our help and happy with her life, there was another side to her. When she got into her moody and defiant mode, no one could convince her of anything. Maybe the person we thought we knew had never existed. Certainly the Martha we knew would never have killed herself.

I thought about Martha's life and wondered about her previous near-death experiences. She had almost died three times when she was young: from a blood transfusion at birth, a serious bout with mononucleosis at five and one year later, a near-fatal reaction to an antibiotic. Although she'd survived these crises, could they have caused permanent damage?

We always considered Martha to be flaky in the sort of way that makes you want to knock on somebody's head and ask, "Is anyone in there?" When she was young, she had a knack for tuning out the world and enjoying herself in her own little cocoon. She used to sit in bed early Saturday mornings before anyone was awake and sing "Kumbaya." It wasn't so much her singing that was odd, but rather the way she looked while she sung, as if she were in a trance, rocking side to side. She went into that same mode when she sat in front of the TV for hours, immersing herself in its fantasy world of heroes and happy endings. After Vita and Angela introduced her to Elvis Presley movies, they became her favorite.

As she got older, other incidents established her quirky character. Like the time at the dinner table when she was shaking her hand in the air, asking Joe, "Where's my fork? I just had it!"

Joe looked at her with a big smile and said, "Martha, look in your hand. You're holding it."

On another occasion, when she was about nineteen, she stood in front of the washing machine, reading the directions, and actually asked me if it was a top-loading or front-loading model. The best Martha story I remember is when she drove me to the airport and wanted to know why she should take me to the Departures ramp when we were, in fact, arriving!

As the plane landed in New York I realized these memories of Martha were all I had left of her. I wasn't sure they were real anymore. I wasn't sure they were Martha. There was no logical segue into what had happened because the Martha I knew had shown no signs of being troubled, depressed or suicidal. Maybe she wasn't just flaky, I thought. Maybe her problem went a lot deeper.

Without Joe to sustain me, I don't think I would've been able to get off the plane. Joe, who had stood by me through all the ups and downs of Vita's illness, was beside me once again, ready to face my family's latest crisis. He really didn't deserve this.

His father Ernie picked us up at the airport. As soon as he saw us, he burst into tears and so did we. He drove us to my old home where Vita, Tommy and Angela were waiting.

Real Life Lesson: Sometimes the people you're closest to turn out to be strangers.

Unsolved Mysteries

After Martha's death, we tried to put the pieces of the puzzle together. We wanted answers. We wanted to know why she had done it. In her bedroom, we found a notebook from a college philosophy course she was taking. Tucked into the back of the book was a short essay for which she had received an A. This surprised me, since she struggled to get B's and C's despite studying for hours. She had changed schools and majors at least three times in the last three years. In the essay, she interpreted the meaning of Socrates' statement, "The unexamined life is not worth living." Her answer gave us a key to her state of mind.

> What he is trying to say is that if you live with a mask on all your life, people do not know you for who you really are. They only see what you want them to see. Therefore, this isn't your real inner self. What people see (the mask) is not worth living because it is a dishonesty that you have with yourself. It is only other people's expectations of you. That mask you portray outside is unexamined, because it really isn't you, and therefore, it is not worth living because that fakeness will prevent you from being independent and honest with yourself...

Was Martha talking about herself in her essay? Did she wear a mask in life? If she did, she never broke character, for I never imagined that she was anyone other than the person she appeared to be. Could this attempt at self-analysis have driven her over the edge? At the time, I wondered if there was a connection between the essay and her suicide. Had she examined herself only to decide her life was not worth living?

Right after Martha's death, Angela combed Martha's bedroom for clues, even after the police had found nothing. Without knowing why, she went immediately to Martha's wastebasket, where she found dozens of torn-up pieces of paper in Martha's handwriting. She spent several hours reassembling the pages and taping them back together. When I arrived the next day, I read them aloud with Angela, Dad and Ma. Martha's letter began with fragments from "Somewhere Over the Rainbow" from *The Wizard of Oz*.

Somewhere over the rainbow, way up high, there's a land that I heard of, once in a lullaby. Somewhere over the rainbow, blue birds fly, birds fly over the rainbow, why, oh why can't I? Where troubles melt like lemon drops away above the chimney tops oh why, oh why can't I?

Sometimes I wish my life would change. I often wonder about another place, somewhere high that is supposed to be heaven. I wish that I could be in this place. My life just seems to get worse as the years go on. My excellent mask allowed no one to know how I really feel and the problems that I am experiencing, for I would never dare tell anyone. I am stubborn and unselfish. I must solve and deal with things on my own. Whether these things are good or evil, my pride and reputation become shaky if I allow anyone inside the mask to help me.

I grew up fast for my age, only to learn that I didn't experience enough fun. I concentrated too much on work and money, which is the heart of my main problems today. I'm insecure in finding something I like to do. Who knows? I might never be satisfied with a job position. I am capable of doing anything I put my mind to, but once I've accomplished the task, I become bored, not giving myself the time in my present job to make money sincerely.

My family life continues to get worse. The fact that I am unable to be on my own affects my pride very deeply. If my father didn't have to worry about me, he would have one less thing to worry about. Between my mother's healthcare and money needed for retirement, he doesn't need a 24-year-old daughter without a career.

Yes, I am sort of the black sheep of the family. I've made all the wrong decisions. God forbid my parents ever knew the things that I have done. Some I regret. Some I don't. However, the ones I regret would be the ones that they would never understand. I think of myself as an intelligent person with common sense but the incidents that I regret make me wonder about myself. How could I have been so stupid? Maybe it was too much pressure for me to handle. This last mess that I'm in I may not get out of. I don't know if I can handle the consequences, which will ruin my career and family.

My boyfriend would do anything for me but I don't think he would forgive me for this one. I could never tell him. This makes me think that maybe he is the wrong guy for me. I should not be afraid to tell him anything; however, since the beginning, I've lied to him about my past and continue to lie to him about my whereabouts. When two people love each other, they are supposed to forgive each other. We have opposite personalities, which is why I don't understand why I stuck with him. Maybe he was manipulating me all along and I never realized it. He does that well. Most of our arguments are about his treatment of me. He hurts me a lot. His way of thinking is evil and it worries me. I've tried to break up with him, but in the end, I give in. His fatal attraction to me scares me. He is one of my major mistakes.

Sometimes I can't take it. I want to end my life so that I won't have any more problems or worries. If I had poison to put in my cup that would instantly kill me, I would do it. I hesitate to use other methods because I don't have the guts. I fear that I will attempt and not succeed, therefore coming back with an even bigger problem. If I am pushed against a wall, I feel I will attempt something. I can't experience anymore sadness, pain, and damage of reputation with my family, boyfriend, and friends. On the other side, I don't want to leave with people knowing I committed suicide. It would be perfect if I got killed in a car accident. My reputation of being a fast driver would justify that. If I'm going to go, I want people to remember me for the way I was.

If I don't have the guts to do it, I can run away to an island or another country and start over. No one would know me. No one would know anything about my family. I would feel free. I would have no trouble to deal with, and I would not make the same mistakes again. Sometimes I wish I could forget the past, have a brain blackout, and just start over.

I don't feel I am a bad person. I have a lot of good in me. I am very caring towards other people and think of them before myself. However, I thought only of myself when I made three major mistakes in my life. It was like the devil took me over in those moments. Sometimes I don't know what's right and what's wrong anymore and want someone else to do the thinking for me. Sometimes I think that all my stress has made me insane and caused me to make bad decisions. This world that I call hell is not good to me. I continue to get deeper and deeper into the claws of the devil because of my mistakes. I can no longer stand it.

I am tired and want to leave this world, my family, and my friends. They will get on with their lives without me. But, do I really want to leave? This problem is the icing on the cake that has pushed me up against a wall. It is affecting my whole life, even though I act happy all day, inside I want to kill myself. Maybe I am better off gone. They say the afterlife is paradise. Maybe I could earn my wings and come back to earth to help people. I like helping people. If only I could help myself.

I think about paradise over the rainbow more so now because I feel I've been pushed too far to the wall. The wall is on fire and I've touched it. It takes faith and sanity to come back. I don't know if I can come back. Half of me wants to and the other half doesn't. What am I to do? I pray so much hoping that I'm worrying for nothing and everything will work out. What will happen to me? Will I actually go insane from all of this? I really don't know. Does anyone exist that will help me understand my situation? Time will tell what will become of me. It may be good or it may be evil. Either way, I will be peaceful. God, I need you to guide me.

Who was the person who had written this letter? If I didn't know Martha's handwriting, I would never have believed she wrote it. This was definitely not my sister. At least not the sister I had known. This was a person she never intended us to know, even after she was dead.

Martha had given us no clue anything was wrong. I must have spoken with her on the phone at least three times in those final two weeks and there had not been a hint of any problem. Two days before her death, Angela spent Easter Sunday with the family. Martha's mood was cheery and she was dressed beautifully, sporting a brand new haircut and outfit. Had she already made her decision by then? Had she already written that letter to herself? There was no way of knowing. She had always been impulsive. She had trouble making up her mind and that led her to make bad decisions, but I couldn't imagine her making this one.

We never found out what Martha's "three major mistakes" were. In her note, she specifies her boyfriend was one of them. From talking with her teachers, friends and employers, we learned she was in a verbally and physically abusive relationship with her boyfriend, that she had been skipping school and had been fired from her last job for stealing money.

Given our upbringing, I'm certain that one of her biggest regrets was having taken money that did not belong to her. Stealing and lying were the two most forbidden offenses in our house. I remember being punished when I was six years old for taking two cents off Tommy's dresser. It didn't matter that the pennies were virtually worthless to him. What mattered was that I took something that wasn't mine to take. When he confronted me, I told the truth to avoid getting spanked, but it didn't make me any less ashamed and embarrassed.

Although suicide seemed totally irrational to us, it was now clear that her pain had been unbearable to Martha. Her emotions had slowly swallowed her up, blocking out the light from the rest of the world, preventing her from finding her way out. She had struggled with the decision to live or die and we would never know what ultimately took her to the wrong door.

That first night in New York after reading Martha's letter, I wanted to drift into a deep sleep and wake up to find it was all a dream. I knew sleep wouldn't come easily and so did Vita. She suggested Angela and I take one of her valiums. Leave it to Vita, I thought, to be offering us an addictive prescription drug like it was chocolate. Of course, this was the same woman who used to give us teaspoons of a home-made whiskey and honey concoction when we had sore throats.

Angela and I hesitated to take the valium, not knowing if we would ever wake up, but we weren't stupid. We knew we needed drugs that night and it took us all of about ten seconds to accept Vita's generous offer. Before I fell into the comforting embrace of the tiny yellow pill that would take me far, far away, I said my prayers. I didn't pray to God that night. I had nothing to say to Her/Him. I prayed instead to Martha.

Martha, I'm so sorry. I never knew what was going on. How did it get so bad? Why didn't you ever say anything? You know I would have helped you.

I've always helped you all your life. Why didn't you come to me? Why didn't I see it? How stupid and selfish I was, all wrapped up in my own life and career. I should have figured out something was wrong.

I'm so sorry I left you in New York alone. I thought you had everything under control, that you were happy. Ma must have driven you crazy with all her orders and demands. It was too much for you. I should have stayed. Then maybe this wouldn't have happened.

I miss you already. I don't think I can stand to live without you. I want to hear your voice, touch your skin, see your face. Come to me in my dreams. Tell me what happened.

Nothing in life seems important anymore. Why bother? It doesn't make any sense. I hope that you are finally at peace and happy.

Real Life Lesson: You can't always save the people who are most precious to you.

Where Was the Cry for Help?

The first time I learned about suicide was in my ninth grade sociology class. I remember reading that most suicide attempts are blatant cries for help, never intended to succeed. Suicidal people usually provide us with obvious clues, such as giving away all their belongings, falling into a deep depression or stating that they don't want to live anymore. This confirms what I had always known to be true: textbooks don't teach us much about real life and all those perfect grades I got didn't mean I'd actually learned anything useful.

Martha's suicide did not match the textbook theories I had learned about in school. It was not a cry for help. There were no warning signs and no previous attempts. Family, friends, co-workers and even her boyfriend were all equally shocked and bewildered.

On the night she died, Martha was supposed to be going to class. Before she left the house, she went into Dad's bedroom, unlocked his gun cabinet and took his revolver. Then she took two bullets from another closet where he kept his ammunition. She purposely chose the kind that explode on impact. These were typically used in hunting, to prevent an animal from suffering longer than necessary.

Dad was a gun collector and an avid hunter who was obsessive about gun safety. He had taught all of us how to use guns but, most importantly, he taught us to stay away from them. His guns were kept unloaded, under lock and key, and we knew never, under any circumstances, to touch them.

With the revolver and bullets hidden on her, she said goodbye to Ma and Dad and drove an hour away to a deserted military airstrip parking lot. I remember having an urge to speak with her that night but when I called, Vita told me she had already left for school. The lot was just minutes away from Angela's home. Had Martha planned to go there first to say goodbye or to ask Angela for help? We'll never know. Angela wasn't home at that time and there were no messages left on her answering machine.

Sometime after she had shot herself, a military employee noticed her car in the middle of the lot. When he saw what had happened, he called the paramedics. She was unconscious but still alive when they got there. They worked on her for twenty minutes, and then her heart stopped. They were amazed she held on as long as she did, but Martha was an avid exerciser with a strong, healthy body. The autopsy showed no evidence of drugs, alcohol, pregnancy or foul play.

Time and time again I've imagined her in that parking lot and wondered what was going through her mind. Was she crying, angry or emotionless? Did she pull the trigger by accident? Did she even think for a second what impact it would have on the rest of the family? Did she know we loved her and that we would do anything to help? How could she hate herself so much that she would take her own life in such a violent way?

That last moment of her life makes me think of a scene in *It's A Wonderful Life* when George Bailey, played by Jimmy Stewart, is about to kill himself by jumping off a bridge. As he's about to jump, an angel named Clarence jumps in first, knowing that George will try to save him—allowing Clarence to save George.

I believe we all have angels around us like Clarence who watch over us and guide us. I wonder what happened to Martha's angels that night. Was her will to die so strong that even an angel could not intercede?

God! Where the hell were you! You are supposed to be there in our time of need. How could you let her life go to waste? After everything we've been through, why this? It kills me like a knife to see the look of pain in Ma and Dad's eyes. Martha only died once but we're dying a thousand deaths. I can't stand it. Take Ma and Dad, please. Put them out of their misery. I'll learn to live with mine but I know they can't get through this. They've been through too much already.

God, I believe there's a reason for everything that happens but I can't see past my anger and pain. I'm grateful that she didn't survive the bullet only to become brain dead for the rest of her life, but why should I be grateful for that? I've had faith and hope for the last six years throughout all of our suffering and what did it get me? This? A dead sister! This is bullshit! Life is bullshit! I want Martha back!

Real Life Lesson: You can only help someone when you know there's a problem.

Somewhere Over
the Rainbow

The days leading up to Martha's funeral were a blur. My body was going through the necessary motions, but my mind and spirit were elsewhere. Relatives had come to stay with us and the house was constantly packed with people. Angela and Aunt Yolanda slept in Martha's bedroom. Joe slept at his parents' house a few miles away. I was sleeping on the living room couch with my cousin Arthur on the floor beside me.

I wanted to be alone to clear my mind but everything I saw or heard reminded me of Martha. Even in the shower, I couldn't escape. The sound of the water transformed itself into the tune of "Somewhere Over the Rainbow," while the chorus repeated in my mind: *Somewhere over the rainbow, way up high, there's a land that I heard of, once in a lullaby. Somewhere over the rainbow, blue birds fly, birds fly over the rainbow, why, oh why can't I?*

The song was soothing and entrancing, although filled with sorrow. I longed for that imaginary place as Martha had, somewhere to take me away from my nightmare. The hot water streaming down my face washed away the salt of my tears, but couldn't reach the pain in my heart.

For the first time in my life I really wanted to be someone or some place else. I suddenly understood how Martha felt. California had been my escape three years earlier: the yellow brick road leading me somewhere sunny and bright, filled with color, and far away from the mental agony and bodily suffering of Vita's illness. I had the good fortune to be attached and yet detached. California was the Oz waiting for me each time I left the darkness of New York. I used to joke that the sun never shined in New York. Maybe it was just my state of mind, but each time I got off the plane in New York, I felt engulfed by the thick, heavy air that suddenly descended upon me like a bad dream. Martha must have felt this way and chosen death as the only means of getting to Oz.

The Wizard of Oz was one of our favorite movies as children. Angela, Martha and I memorized most of the dialogue and would act out scenes even as adults. If Martha had to choose a song to represent her, it would have to have been either "Somewhere Over the Rainbow" or an Elvis song. Given the situation, "Hound Dog" or "Love Me Tender" didn't match her despair like the famous song that gave us the image of a lost young girl longing for happiness and love. But how could Martha have completely forgotten the lessons we learned from the movie? It was as if she only remembered the first few scenes in black-and-white. She forgot the part that shows you running away is not the answer and that each of us has the power within ourselves to find happiness.

A couple of days after Martha's death, Angela and I met with the funeral director to make arrangements. Ma and Dad were too sick and disabled to deal with it. Pat Foyder's daughter Patricia, who was one of Martha's best friends, came along to give us support. We could barely speak in answer to the director's questions. I couldn't believe I was being asked what to do with the body of my sister who two weeks before had been alive and well.

He offered to show us her body but we immediately declined. We could not bear to see her, especially since we knew her face would be disfigured from the bullet wound to the head. We decided to cremate her and have her ashes saved at the funeral home until another family member died. Angela and I somehow knew that's what Martha would have wanted and I wondered if she had ever told us this. Vita and Tommy were not in favor of cremation at first, but when the church approved it, they acquiesced. We gave the funeral director an 8x10 picture of Martha to place on top of her closed coffin during the services.

Hundreds of friends, family and co-workers came to pay their respects at the funeral home. The pitiful scene was devastating to everyone. Vita and Tommy were front and center in their wheelchairs, sobbing as each guest came up to see them. Tommy especially, with his empty stare and nearby crutches, was a pitiful reminder of a man who had once been the pillar of strength in the family. Angela and I roamed around, teary-eyed, greeting people we hadn't seen for years. We kept glancing at the picture of Martha smiling ear-to-ear, and wondered what went wrong.

They say that everyone has a mission in life and that people who commit suicide abort that mission. When they die, they realize they can't escape their fate but must still learn their remaining lessons. Whenever I hear "Somewhere Over the Rainbow" I think of Martha. I believe she is in a place like Oz with spirits who are helping her find her way back home.

Dear God, I pray for Martha's soul. I'm afraid she is tormented in death, as she was in life. Please help her grow. Please forgive her. Please forgive all of us.

I don't know why I'm here on earth and why my family has suffered so much. Please give me the strength to understand.

I don't want to blame myself. I'm sorry I want to blame anyone. I want to blame Ma for her relentless demands, and Dad for his hard criticism, and Martha's boyfriend for his abusive nature and Angela for her lack of involvement. And of course, me—for not being there, for not taking care of her. We probably all had something to do with it. I'm so sorry.

Was she crazy all along? I'd like to believe that. Or that it was just "her time to go," as they say, and she would have died that day anyway. I'd like to believe that because it takes away the guilt.

Whoever you are out there, please help Martha. Please help us all.

Real Life Lesson: When you feel compelled to blame everyone and no one at the same time, pray for inner peace.

Things That Matter

The first task after the funeral and the thank-you cards that Vita insisted we send, was to go through Martha's belongings and figure out what to do with them. Of course, Vita delegated this task to Angela and me: the only two people in the house physically able to do it. Little did we know we would hone this exercise to perfection over the next four years—although this first time was to be the most difficult.

Angela and I wanted to throw everything away as fast as we could, thinking that by removing every trace of Martha from the house, we would remove the pain as well. We used this same concept when we had her ashes boxed up—as if we could contain her life and tragic death, and our memories and guilt, in one neat little package and hide it away from sight. We were so afraid of what would happen to us if we actually felt all of our pain.

I wanted to control Martha's ashes just as I had controlled everything else in my life. I had figured out how to control Vita's situation by putting it in a separate compartment in my brain, far away from everything else—the good stuff in my life. Martha's death was uncontrollable, a mystery with unanswered questions. Ashes have a tendency to scatter, float and touch down on everything. They were all over her stuff.

Each garment, each shoe, each piece of jewelry made us stop and look, touch and smell, as we tried to hold onto any piece of Martha still clinging to it. We found a photo of Martha when she was five years old, in her tap dance costume. We decided that she was the cutest of us all. But we thought maybe this was because Vita had finally stopped giving us home permanents by the time Martha arrived!

We felt guilty about taking anything, as if we were stealing Martha's personal belongings. Angela would insist I keep an item and I would insist she keep it. These were the same items we would have fought over as teenagers.

Vita used to make us share our clothes. She would say, "Don't fight with your sister. You're gonna want her around when you get older."

"But Ma, she's gonna stretch it out and I won't be able to wear it again!"

How insignificant those fights and those things seemed now that Martha was gone. How insignificant everything seemed.

Real Life Lesson: Don't confuse the value of material things with the people you love, for the one is worthless and the other is priceless.

Facing Your Demons

I stayed in New York with Vita and Tommy for a month after Martha died. Joe went back to work in California weeks ahead of me. Every time I got close to leaving, there was another crisis to handle or another job to do. In some ways, I wanted an excuse to stay because I couldn't imagine leaving my parents alone.

A week after the funeral, Vita was in the hospital with pneumonia. Knowing Dad would need help even after Vita came home, we hired a middle-aged Polish man with the strength of an ox, who spoke enough English to understand what we needed. We also hired a young woman to handle the grocery shopping, cleaning and household chores Martha had done. She could also fill in for Vita's regular nurses, since she had some nursing skills.

During the first couple of months after Martha's suicide, we talked about her incessantly. We reminisced about how she acted and looked. We had an insatiable desire to reconstruct the weeks before she died. We recounted the last conversations, moods, phone calls, photographs and meals, hoping that somehow our memories would explain the answer to why she'd killed herself. That question still gnawed at our guts, creating a big, black, empty hole.

We craved closure but were never satisfied. I wondered if that was because we never saw Martha's body. For months, I dreamt it was all a mistake and had never happened. Martha returned in my dreams to explain that she had simply taken a long trip. Overcome with the sight of her alive, I would wake up crying with joy, my pillow wet with tears. After a few minutes I'd realize it was only a dream.

On other nights, I was haunted by an image of Martha with a bloody face and distorted head, as if she'd come right out of a horror movie—back from the dead, to get her revenge on those who had failed her.

We went through all the textbook stages of grief from denial to anger to sorrow. Sooner or later, we all settled into the same place: the end of the road where the demons of guilt were waiting for us.

Dad and Ma didn't have to tell me. I knew how they were feeling. Dad asked me why Martha hadn't come to him when she was in trouble. Although I didn't want to pour salt on his wounds, I told him the truth. He was the last person we would go to if we were in trouble for fear of disappointing him, shaming ourselves or suffering the consequences of his anger. I reminded him how afraid I was to come home after being bitten by a dog when I was eight years old.

Deep down, in my subconscious, I wanted to hurt him by telling him this. As a father, he hadn't exactly been involved in our lives. I wanted to ask him, "Where were you? Where were you when Angela and I were helping Martha with her homework all those years? Where were you when Ma saw her teachers? You might've figured something out before it was too late. She did, after all, live under your roof. This didn't happen overnight."

I chose not to twist the knife after I had already stabbed him and I felt terrible for saying what little I did. He never responded, which scared the hell out of me. I tried to make amends by saying I knew that he meant well and was just trying to protect us from getting hurt.

Then I asked myself why Martha hadn't come to Angela or me. Were our standards so high that she couldn't bring herself to explain her feelings or her mistakes? In her letter she was clearly contemplating suicide but, at the same time, she wasn't one hundred percent convinced it was the answer to her problems. Was there something Angela and I could have noticed that would've enabled us to stop her?

When I went back to California, I could only operate on one of two extreme levels. Either I completely broke down at the mention of Martha's name or I detached myself from the entire incident—as if I were a broadcaster reporting a news story. I could only get away with the latter approach when addressing business associates or casual acquaintances. The conversation would go something like this:

> Them: So, how's your family?
> Me: Okay, except I just lost my younger sister.
> Them: Oh, I'm so sorry. How did it happen?
> Me: She killed herself. *(Silence. I know I've caught them off guard and they don't know how to respond.)*
> Them: Did she have problems? Did you know this would happen? How did she do it?
> Me: No, she gave us no warning. She just shot herself.

I could have this conversation without emotion, just explaining the facts, with people who didn't know me well, but when it came to talking to someone close, like Joe or Aunt Yolanda, my emotions would swing like a pendulum to the other extreme. Poor Joe had to deal with it daily. I sometimes tried to spare Aunt Yolanda the inevitable river of tears by not seeing her or not taking her calls. I knew she understood.

When I was alone, my emotions got the best of me. While driving my car to a business appointment, I would start crying uncontrollably. Several times I had to pull over onto the side of the road to clear my eyes and fix my face. It only took one single thought of Martha to set me off. I began to hate darkness. I left a night-light on because I was frightened of being greeted by Martha's gruesome, bloody face on one of my trips to the bathroom.

I usually went to bed before Joe but I didn't want to be left alone, so Joe brought a small portable TV into the bedroom to watch while I drifted off to sleep. God bless Joe! I knew I was being irrational but I couldn't get over it. Maybe it was my own image I was afraid to see in the mirror at night. Maybe I would see clear through my head to my soul and my feelings of guilt.

After about four months, the family stopped talking about Martha. Vita and Tommy seldom brought up her name, for fear of re-opening wounds that had bled so profusely for months. Since it was more painful to watch each other suffer than to suffer by ourselves, we made an unconscious decision to suffer alone. Martha's death had revealed depths of sadness that we had never displayed to each other as a family. Laughter, at appropriate moments, had always been welcome in our house but crying never had its place.

On top of their grief, Ma and Dad seemed embarrassed by what Martha had done. When Angela announced her plans to get divorced, they had urged her to make her marriage work—not because they thought the marriage was worth saving, but because divorce was against their religious beliefs. Martha's suicide had the same effect. They were embarrassed by the stigma they thought would fall upon them and our family. They were afraid people would think their daughter was crazy or, even worse, that they had made her crazy!

Soon after returning to California, I was back in a regular routine at work. I was offered a promotion from sales to management that I had worked hard to get. My new responsibilities of hiring, training and motivating my new team kept me busy. The nights, however, were still filled with demons that continued to haunt me.

I lost ten pounds because I couldn't eat without feeling sick to my stomach. Watching Fourth of July fireworks, I thought I would never again enjoy any celebration in life. The emotional pain was suffocating me. Three months after Martha's death, I felt worse than the day she'd died. I began to worry I would be emotionally scarred by this event forever, that my even-tempered personality would take a hit. I knew my soul was still heavy with guilt and I decided to get help.

My general doctor recommended a therapist who specialized in family counseling. She was a perfect fit for me: a Jewish ex-New Yorker—about the closest thing you can get to an Italian ex-New Yorker. She understood the family dynamics in my household: the drama, the respect demanded and the relationships.

In the back of my rational mind, I had already decided that no one was to blame. I just needed a little help to bring that thought to the forefront of my emotions. Over a three-month period I met with the therapist once a week and we talked about everything from the family environment growing up, to my parents' and sisters' personalities, to my dreams.

It's amazing how the scenes in the dreams seemed to mirror what I was feeling. In many of them, I was trying to care for Martha (whether that meant giving her cookies to eat, dressing her or taking her places) but I was upset because she wasn't cooperating. This was the key. I always felt responsible for her and when she killed herself, I felt responsible for that too. As if I'd failed her.

Slowly, the therapist allowed me to shed my guilt and sorrow and move towards forgiveness. Some people are amazed that this all happened in only about twelve sessions but it did. By the end of the third month, I didn't feel I needed to see her and she felt the same. Completely in line with my character, I had set a goal for myself and achieved it in record time! Then, I put it behind me and moved on.

I knew our parents would not be open to outside help, so I never broached the subject with them. However, I did try to share anything I had learned in therapy that I thought would make them feel better. For example, telling them Martha had probably been dyslexic helped explain a struggle that may have started as far back as grammar school. Reassuring them that they were good parents who had done the best they could was also important to me.

Only years later did I discover things that shed more light on Martha's state of mind. She had been pregnant more than once and was suffering from post-abortion syndrome, which affects some women. Symptoms include withdrawal, self-devaluation, guilt and depression. Martha also had an eating disorder and was bulimic the last two years of her life. Bulimia both stems from and induces self-destructive feelings and behavior. Both of these disorders, which put many young women's lives at risk, can easily go unnoticed. Tommy and Vita weren't around to benefit from these revelations.

Memories of Martha will always be in my heart but as time goes on, I have to struggle to keep their fading images alive inside of me. I look at photographs of her to remind myself of her face and I try to remember the sound of her voice. Somewhere along my journey, amid the hate I felt towards Martha for what she did and the hate I felt towards myself for not being there to help, I learned the lessons of forgiveness and love. I stopped judging and blaming myself, Martha, or anyone else, and I accepted the situation for what it was. I knew in my heart God forgives all and loves all and that I could too.

Dear God, thank you for guiding me to peace in my heart, to forgiveness and to healing. Thank you for your love and the love of all my family, especially Joe who has been by my side throughout, never wavering in his love for me, never being selfish, never asking me when I'll get over this. In my worst moments, he has shown me what love really is.

Dear Martha, I forgive you. I forgive myself. I forgive Ma and Dad and Angela and anyone else I thought might have contributed to that fatal night. I pray that you find your way to happiness and peace. I will pray for you every day. Thank you for showing me what matters most in life: love. I will never forget you. You will always be my funny, quirky, moody, beautiful baby sister whom I will love eternally.

Real Life Lesson: Together, love and forgiveness are the golden keys to a peaceful soul and a happy heart.

Martha (5 years old) as an angel
1971

III

TOMMY

How Much is Too Much?

I was sure the pneumonia brought on by Martha's death would kill Vita and I was prepared for her to die. Death would put an end to six years of misery—but Vita didn't seem to see it that way. She wasn't ready to leave this world. She bounced back from near-death pneumonia as she had many times before, surprising even herself. When she said she didn't know why God didn't take her, we jokingly replied that there wasn't enough room in heaven for both Martha and Vita. Pat Foyder said Martha didn't want Vita up there because she would put her to work!

Angela and I worried about our parents and how they were coping with Martha's death. Martha's suicide suddenly made the last six years of trauma seem benign in comparison. It was the difference between living through a series of small tremors over a period of years, where each one takes a little bit more out of you, and surviving a major earthquake with enormous destruction and loss resulting from one big jolt.

We decided to create a diversion for our parents by throwing a family birthday party with a handful of friends. Both of their birthdays were in July. Vita's was on the 28th, which made her a Leo, and Tommy's on the 10th, which made him a Cancer—completely opposite personalities. Leo is the proud lion: outgoing, gregarious, opinionated, the life of the party. Cancer is crabby, moody and shy, the ultimate homebody. My birthday fell right in between, July 21, on the cusp between Cancer and Leo. I think that's why I knew how to play both sides.

During the party, Vita was in her social glory, surrounded by friends, but Tommy looked like he wanted to crawl into a hole. He was quiet, pale and withdrawn throughout the evening, flashing a phony smile as needed. We figured the recent stress of Martha's death had probably slowed his recovery from hip surgery.

Naturally, we thought the worst was over and there couldn't possibly be any more bad luck coming our way, but fate was preparing to say, "Ha! Gotcha again when you weren't looking!" A month after the July birthday party and just four months after Martha died, we were reminded how little control we really have over God's master plan. Tommy was diagnosed with multiple myeloma: bone marrow cancer.

Unlike the first two family crises, this piece of bad news didn't shock me. I knew this was Tommy's demon finally rising to the surface. In the last few years he had lost the lifestyle to which he was accustomed; Vita was more of a burden to him than a wife; his life savings were depleted; his home was invaded by strangers and—just when it seemed like things couldn't get worse—his daughter had used his gun to take her life.

I knew he blamed himself for Martha's death and this cancer was his self-punishment. I don't think most cancer is self-inflicted, but I do think Tommy's was. I knew we all had cancer cells in our bodies and medical science had not yet determined why they grow in some people and not in others. Obviously, emotional distress lowers the immune system and leaves the body open for an invasion of bad cells. Aside from the stress, I truly believed my father did not want to live anymore.

I spoke with him on the phone the day I found out. "You know, Dad, you did this to yourself."

"Yes, I know."

"I know you can beat it," I said, "if you try."

"Yes, I know."

I wondered how much trauma one family could handle. Then I realized we had survived a great deal and would survive this as well, day by day.

God, I know you've been testing us, but I think it's gone overboard now. I don't blame you for Dad's illness. I know he wanted this; he willed it to happen. But help him through it. I can't imagine you would take him from us. Ma would never survive. I hate Dad for this. I hate his weakness. He's chosen anger and bitterness to deal with Ma's situation all these years and now he's checking-out completely. I pray he'll have the strength to fight this. He's always had Ma to take care of him and now she can't. He's got to help himself, but I'm not sure he can.

Real Life Lesson: Rid yourself of guilt, which serves only to kill your body, mind and spirit.

Tommy George

With Vita, what you saw was what you got. Tommy was much more complicated. Although he was an intelligent man of many talents, if you didn't know him well, you'd think he was just a simple blue-collar worker. He never boasted about himself. The only evidence of a multi-dimensional character was his temperament, which could change him from a charming husband and father to a raging bull in a matter of seconds.

Tommy wasn't as forthcoming about his past as Vita. Maybe it was just the difference between how men and women communicate (or don't). Or maybe he was just a very private person who didn't want to relive an unhappy childhood. Either way, you had to pull the stories out of him bit by bit to catch a glimpse of his childhood.

Born in 1925, Tommy grew up during the Depression on a self-sufficient farm in upstate New York. His family churned their own butter, grew their own vegetables and ate what meat they could hunt. All five children worked hard on the farm. Tommy was the eldest and Yolanda was the only girl. His parents came from Italy. His father Arturo was an ignorant, illiterate man who ruthlessly beat his wife and children. His personality was so unpleasant that once they were adults, his children would simply banish him from their lives for long periods of time.

Tommy usually gave in, forgave his father and invited him back into our home. I think he did it out of love for his mother, who'd been a saint for putting up with Arturo all those years. She died of a heart attack when I was seven and Arturo moved in with one of his long-term mistresses. He died when I was in my teens. I'll always remember Grandpa Gisonni as this crazy little bald guy who fought with everyone, drank too much and called me Bebbie.

After high school, Tommy enlisted in the Marines but was soon dismissed because of an inner ear problem dating from childhood. He returned to his family in New York City, where they'd moved after the Depression.

The only memorable stories Tommy told us about growing up were those he used as examples of things we shouldn't do. Like the time he got trapped in a barn fire, which made him paranoid about fires getting started. He used to make us unplug every electrical appliance and lamp before we left the house. We learned at an early age not to play with matches and unfortunately, it worked so well that to this day I still can't light one!

Then there was the story about falling through the ice in winter, which kept us away from frozen ponds for most of our lives. I did finally learn to ice skate at an indoor rink. The most vivid story was about his nine-year-old brother dying after being hit by a car while playing softball in the street. Needless to say, we were forbidden to cross a street without at least one parent holding our hand until we were in our teens.

These incidents formed his Don't/you'll collection of teachings. Don't put barrettes in your hair, you'll fall and cut your head open. Don't drive in the rain, you'll get into an accident. Don't go on the school trip to New York City, you'll be mugged. Don't go out with your hair wet, you'll catch pneumonia. Don't go to fashion design school, you'll never find a job! Don't talk to strangers, you'll be taken away! (Okay, there were some good tips in there, but his fear of potential danger was obsessive.)

Most children are curious about their parents' lives before they were parents. What did they look like? What trouble did they get into? How did they act? The answers usually paint the picture of people who are quite different from the parents they become. We didn't know a whole lot about Tommy's childhood but Vita told us stories about him from when they met. He definitely seemed like a happier, more fun-loving person back then.

His dream in life had been to act and sing, although his parents gave this no support or encouragement. He adopted the Americanized stage name Tommy George and took acting classes in the evenings, while working as a cutter in New York's garment industry during the day. Five years of auditions and training got him a few parts in off-Broadway plays and a singing gig at Carnegie Hall. He took one trip to Hollywood to pursue a film career but mild earthquake tremors on his first night sent him right back to New York. He had an old scrapbook with all his reviews and publicity photos that we used to love looking through when we were kids. The reviews were quite good. One paper called him "a combination of Sinatra and Clark Gable with a dash of Humphrey Bogart in his hard-boiled technique."

Once he and Vita got married, four years after they met, he gave up acting for good, knowing it was not the kind of work that would enable him to provide for his wife and family. For a couple of years, he left the garment industry to sell custom portraits for a photography firm, but the company went out of business.

Before they had children, Tommy took two years off to write a play while Vita worked as a seamstress. The play was about a boxer who was torn between his love of boxing, his mother and a femme fatale. When it didn't sell, he went back to the cutting room in the garment district. To keep his dream alive, he began writing songs. They were beautiful love songs like Frank Sinatra or Tony Bennett would sing, but he couldn't sell them. We knew these songs by heart, since he sang them to us when we were growing up. His voice was smooth and operatic, just like his mother's.

In later years he kept his creative juices flowing by inventing things. As a teenager, I'd see him in the kitchen looking like a mad scientist with pots of boiling water on the stove and eggs everywhere. Although he eventually obtained a patent for his hard-boiled-egg—peeler, because his invention worked only under certain conditions, he never made a dime off it.

Tommy was the perfect match for Vita in looks and stature. They made a handsome pair, especially when they were dressed to go out. Vita was always fashionable and Tommy wore a traditional fedora hat well after it went out of style. He had fedoras for every occasion: light-weight for summer, tweed for winter and red wool for hunting.

Although Vita said they'd gone dancing a lot, you would never have guessed it from his behavior at a family wedding. Vita would be the first one on the dance floor, leading the Sicilian tarantella, while Tommy sat waiting until it was time to go home. The pressures of marriage, children and ongoing money problems seemed to have dampened his once jovial personality.

His dreams of show business defeated, Tommy fell back on food, family, hunting and guns. He was in his glory sitting at the dinner table surrounded by his family, with a big plate of pasta in front of him. The plate he used was more like a platter. He frequently had seconds and would finish off anything we left. Those extra helpings showed up on his big round belly.

His other favorite activity was sitting on a tree stump alone in the woods, listening to nature and waiting for a deer to come around the bend. After hunting, he'd spend hours meticulously cleaning and polishing his guns. He loved watching American Sportsman or Animal Kingdom on TV.

Tommy, like many fathers in the 1960s, left the child rearing to the little woman. His responsibility ended with his paycheck. Everything else was left to Vita, including earning extra money to make ends meet.

He was involved in discipline but Vita was the one who was home with us, cooked for us, took us to school and attended all our parent-teacher conferences. Sure, once in a while, he would throw a softball around or take us to get ice cream, but those occasions were few and far between. His interest in kid's stuff peaked with his first child and plummeted soon thereafter when Angela was about seven and I was only four.

The one thing we always did as a family was eat dinner together. As soon as Tommy's car pulled into the driveway, we knew we had to be ready to greet him with a kiss and a set dinner table. Vita had the food on the table within minutes of his arrival. Depending on how his day at work had gone, conversation would range from silence to pleasant talk to loud fights.

After dinner, Tommy would read the paper and then watch the news on TV—the six o'clock and the eleven o'clock news, just in case he missed something! In between, there might be a few TV shows or a movie that we would watch together before going to sleep. During this time between work and bed, he didn't want any interruptions from the outside world, such as people dropping by or phone calls.

When Tommy was home, our objective was to keep him happy, which was a difficult task since his temper could explode over anything. Not physically abusive as his father had been, his booming yell could still make anyone run the other way. We respected and feared him and those were not mutually exclusive emotions. When Vita said, "Your father's in a bad mood," we knew to stay away because anything could set him off.

My girlfriends saw the best side of Tommy: he instantly turned into my charming father, saying things to make them smile or laugh. Boyfriends got a different treatment. Angela's male friends in high school nicknamed him Rocky (a pre-Sylvester Stallone gangsterish name) because every time Angela brought a boy home, Tommy would be cleaning his guns. I'm not sure if he did this consciously or not but it sent a clear message: Mess with my daughter and this is what you'll be facing.

Although Tommy might have acted the gangster part well, underneath he was the most honest, law-abiding person I knew. He condemned all criminal behavior. When he participated in local politics, his extreme honesty and belief in doing things the right way only alienated him from the rest of the politicians.

Tommy was extremely proud of all of us and truly loved us but like Vita, he had a difficult time actually telling us. Disapproval and anger were much easier emotions for him to display than approval and love. When I left home to move to California, his parting message was "Knock 'em dead, Kid." That was his way of telling me he was proud of me and wished me the best in life.

Tommy would have kept us by his side our entire lives if he could have, in order to protect us. Despite having to tip-toe around his volatile temper, I always had a safe feeling when I was home, as if I were in a warm cocoon. He must have been shattered by his inability to prevent the one thing he feared most—losing one of his children.

Real Life Lesson: Remember your parents were once young, with dreams and hopes just like yours.

Bitterness

Tommy's life hadn't exactly turned out as planned. I'm sure he never imagined that he would spend thirty years in ILGWA (International Ladies' Garment Workers of America). It started out as a job to pay the bills until one of his more creative projects took off. At some point, and I don't know when, he gave up on his dreams even though he hated his job. I often wondered what went through his head all those years. I wasn't sure if he had accepted his fate or regretted what he had not attained.

When Vita got sick, the life he probably didn't think was all that great to begin with suddenly got worse. He didn't just lose a wife—he lost a maid, a butler, a cook, a companion and a lover. Dinner wasn't on the table when he got home and his laundry wasn't cleaned and pressed. He was forced to learn how to perform household chores he truly believed only women should do. I remember asking him to buy us a dishwasher when we were in our teens and his reply was, "Why should I buy a dishwasher when I have four already!"

When Vita came home with 24-hour nursing care, he lost the last sacred privilege in his home: his privacy. He would have had to be a different person not to be bitter about his situation. After a lifetime of disappointments, this took him over the edge. His hair-trigger temperament became even more volatile, making him at times downright mean-spirited. He began to resent Vita for being sick, while he struggled with his own pain from a deteriorating hip.

With all he had been through, I really couldn't condemn him. I sometimes felt resentment towards Vita too, but I tried not to show it. Her aggressive, demanding personality was hard enough to swallow when she was healthy. When you have to cater to someone who is sick, you start off with good intentions but, over time, their neediness gnaws on your nerves making you want to scream at them. You hold your tongue only because you know it's incredibly selfish of you to feel that way.

Each time I visited, Tommy seemed increasingly ornery. That loving singer/actor/inventor father I knew was buried far beneath the surface and I wondered if he could ever come back. He didn't even pretend to be cordial when visitors came. Before Martha's death, I decided to have a talk with him, adult to adult. I wasn't sure how to approach this talk since we had never had a discussion like this before.

I asked him to take a drive with me to the store and when we arrived at the parking lot, I calmly told him something was bothering me. I tried to get him to recognize how mean and rude his behavior had become. I told him it was not the way he had brought us up, and it was embarrassing to see him behave like that. I didn't know what to expect. I was glad he didn't start yelling at me. In fact, he said nothing. I know he listened, but I wondered if the message was too little, too late.

Shortly afterwards, he decided to get his hip replacement surgery. A month after the operation, Martha committed suicide. He decided from the beginning that he'd killed her. Four months later, they found the cancer in him. Once he was sick, the bitterness gave way to total withdrawal. He wasn't going to be angry anymore. He wasn't going to fight. He wanted out. His was a life of broken dreams. He had built a huge house of cards with card upon card of failures and lost hopes. Martha's death brought the house down.

Dear God, help my father get his spirit back. I know he doesn't mean to hurt anyone but he does. First he hurt us with his anger and now he's giving up. He's going to leave us holding the bag. Then what will we do with Ma?

He's such a poor, unhappy soul. Maybe he didn't try hard enough in life to make his dreams come true. Maybe they were never meant to be. But why torture him like this? He can get through it. I believe he can. I pray for the cancer to go away. I pray for him to be as strong as I always believed he was.

Ma doesn't understand what's really going on. She still thinks she's worse off than Dad is. Help her to show him the love they once had. Help her to connect with him again. I fear it's too late. Martha's death seems to have driven a wedge into the small piece of connective tissue they still have.

Real Life Lesson: The anger you project onto others can destroy you.

The Green Juice

Vita had introduced us to hospital life, illness and the world of medicine. After her operation, she developed a myriad of health complications that exposed us to an endless array of specialists in areas such as urology, allergy, cardiology, opthamology, pulmonary medicine, dentistry, endocrinology, gastroenterology, neurology and orthopedics.

Vita could have definitely used some help in the area of psychiatry but, of course, she chose to skip that entire field for fear of being labeled crazy. And since her tumor was benign, we had yet to learn about oncology. I suppose our medical education wouldn't have been complete without studying cancer. It was Tommy who introduced us to that part of the curriculum.

Cancer was another one of those things that only happened to people outside our imaginary safe boundary. Once again, we learned that no one is immune to illness. Multiple myeloma is a form of cancer that attacks blood cells produced by the bone marrow. An uncontrollable growth of these cells produces enzymes that destroy bones, causing a multitude of problems such as blood cell damage, anemia, infection, bone tumors and kidney failure. The oncologist told us that this particular form of cancer was *treatable*. At the time, we assumed that meant *curable*. We didn't know the difference.

The only other piece of information the doctors willingly shared was that chemotherapy would have to start immediately. We seemed to forget everything we had learned over the previous six years about the need to ask questions and get involved. It's funny how you have to learn the same lessons over and over again until you get them right.

We never asked for and therefore never got a thorough explanation of my father's disease or the prescribed treatment. Maybe we didn't want to know. It was easier to hear and believe the words *cancer, treatable, chemotherapy.* Maybe after all that had happened to Martha and Vita, we couldn't handle the thought of another loss.

I felt sorry for Tommy but I was also angry with him because I thought the cancer was his way of dealing with Martha's death. He had kept his feelings bottled up until the guilt and sorrow finally overcame him, poisoning his body. That's the way my reasoning went. I needed to believe that. Tommy had brought this life-threatening disease upon himself and, because I believed it was self-inflicted, I wanted him to be able to get rid of it as well. I was sure he was going to beat it and free himself of his demons, just as I had.

Tommy was sixty-five and freshly retired when his chemotherapy began in September 1990. It was right before he and Vita had planned to take their first trip to California to visit me. I'd made arrangements with the airlines for Vita to bring her medical equipment and a nurse on board. It would have been their second vacation trip in thirty-six years of marriage. They never made it.

Vita was slowly returning to a semi-normal state after another hospital stay for pneumonia when Tommy started chemotherapy. God forbid she wasn't the center of attention. She still seemed to be the needier one relative to Tommy. He had a treatment plan that was driven by the doctors, but Vita's only plan was hands on deck at all times, managing the crisis of the day, as her condition was always volatile. She could live another decade or another week. No one knew.

Tommy got treatments on an outpatient basis. I accompanied him on one of his first visits and watched as he lay down on a table with an intravenous tube connected to his arm. The first thing I noticed was the fluid dripping into his veins from the plastic bag. It was lime green! I couldn't believe there were any life-sustaining properties in something that looked like monster bile.

Again I asked myself, "Medicine or mad science?" Apparently, this precise mixture of chemicals was specifically formulated for his type of cancer. For something that had been presented as a relatively painless and benign procedure, it sure looked like a deadly cocktail.

The well-known side effects of chemotherapy, such as hair loss and nausea, seemed like a small price to pay for life but I soon realized that those side effects were just the tip of the iceberg. I began to truly understand the nature of two beasts: cancer and chemotherapy. Most cancer treatment works by eradicating mutated cells and preventing further growth. Since it's not an exact science, it also kills the good cells. Imagine the chaos that is created inside a person's body as the bad cells are overtaking the good cells and the chemo is wiping them all out! It's like an internal hurricane, leveling everything in its path.

Tommy's first couple of treatments left him extremely tired and lethargic. His fedora was replaced with a baseball cap after all of his wavy black hair fell out. As time went on and more chemicals were pumped into him, the corrosive effects of chemotherapy started to conquer his body and spirit. His skin took on a grayish hue and his eyelids drooped as if he were in a drunken stupor.

Weakened limbs made his gait unsteady and a low whisper replaced his booming voice. His voracious appetite died along with his love of food and the pleasure he once derived from sitting down to a good home-cooked meal. He was emotionally distant, talking only when spoken to. When he had a good day or two, it usually meant it was time for another dose of the green juice.

Angela frequently received phone calls from Vita saying that Tommy had to be rushed to the hospital because he was disoriented. One time, Angela stood outside his hospital room door and watched him staring out the window with tears in his eyes. When she came into the room he said, "Angela, who's going to get my car if I die? Who's going to take care of your mother?"

This was the first time he said anything serious about dying. Angela quickly tried to assure him that nobody was going to die and then changed the subject as this wasn't something she was used to discussing. It was a sad, emotionally charged subject that was painful to talk about. We never went there as a family.

About six months into his treatment, I accompanied him on another doctor's visit. I was extremely concerned about his increasing frailty and mentioned this to his doctor, but the doctor insisted that, based on Tommy's latest blood work, he was improving. I wanted to scream at the doctor, "I don't care what your paperwork tells you! Look at the patient, you moron! He looks like he's dying." I didn't. I just watched as he gave him another green cocktail. I prayed silently that the doctor was right and hoped that the old Tommy—the strong and commanding father I loved—would come back again soon.

He would endure about a year of chemotherapy. I never talked to him about the possibility of death and he neither mentioned it nor challenged any of my positive words of encouragement. I assumed he was fighting the good fight. He didn't complain, even though he was obviously in a lot of pain. It was as if he had made a pact with himself to suffer in silence—just as he had after Martha died.

I was no better. I kept my feelings of love for him silent as always. It was so hard for me to tell him I loved him or to hug him. I hadn't hugged him—I mean really hugged—since I was about eight years old. Oh sure, I'd do the obligatory hello-and-goodbye lean-and-kiss but that was about it. Vita and Tommy were never openly affectionate or demonstrative towards each other or us, so it never came easy to me.

I had no problem embracing a friend or even a colleague. Maybe that was because it didn't stir up deep emotional feelings or commitments. I could cry at the drop of a hat during an AT&T commercial or a sappy *Brady Bunch* ending, but I couldn't cry in front of my parents. I was taught to get over it and be strong. I had been taught that there was never a reason to cry.

The whole time Tommy was sick, I talked to him as if I were coaching an athlete. "You can do it, Dad. I know you can." Those words were about as emotional as the phone conversations we had. He would ask, "How's the job?" and I would respond, "Great." Then he would say something about the weather in New York and I would mention the weather in California. Then he would say, "Here's your mother," and hand Vita the phone.

Dear God, why can't I comfort him or free him from the shackles of Martha's death? I fear he's dying alone on his own little island while I'm fighting my own storm in the same sea. I feel so weak myself. I want to throw him a life jacket, but I don't know how. I want to apologize for saying his own daughters couldn't come to him if we were in trouble, but I won't. I want to tell him I love him, but I can't. I'm afraid if I scratch the surface, I'll start crying and never stop.

When I look in his eyes, I wish he could see my feelings like some cartoon bubble above my head because I can't say the words. I'm sorry. What's wrong with me? Please help him find his way out of this.

Real Life Lesson: When you are most afraid to express your emotions is when you most need to.

Turning Thirty

For my thirtieth birthday in 1991, Joe made plans to take me on a romantic four-day trip to Vancouver. The month before, he had lost his grandmother whom he loved dearly and with whom he shared a special relationship. Grammy, as we called her, once confessed to me that Joe was her favorite, although she would never have admitted that to anyone else.

Joe needed the time away as much as I did and we were supposed to leave right after I came back from a New York business trip. After a weekend with my parents, Tommy's condition took a turn for the worse, landing him in the hospital. His oncologist did not think he would make it through this setback. Angela and I actually overheard the doctor say to a nurse, "Is Gisonni still here?"

From the tone of his voice, he didn't mean, "Has he been discharged?" but rather, "Is he dead?" Angela and I did the only thing we could do for our own comfort and peace of mind: we fired him that day and hired another doctor who was more hopeful. During this time, Tommy started to hallucinate. I extended my stay and canceled the Vancouver trip.

On my birthday, I sat in Tommy's hospital room with Angela, watching and listening to the party going on in our father's head. It was quite an entertaining experience. I only wish I'd had some of what he was smoking!

It was the first time I ever thought about how fun it might be to be high on drugs.

I've never had a desire to experiment with drugs, or even cigarettes, for fear of the consequences and, since we grew up drinking homemade wine with dinner and sipping anisette with dessert, alcohol was never a big deal either. I guess the only real vice we all had was an addiction to food. It's an Italian thing.

Tommy was awake: his eyes were open, he was talking, his face was expressive and he knew we were there because he was referring to us by name, but he seemed totally pain-free and happy. And from what we could gather, he saw a lot more people in the room than just Angela and me. He kept talking to friends and relatives (most of whom had passed away) as if they were right there in front of him.

He was joking around and laughing like he didn't have a care in the world. I hadn't seen him laugh like that for years. Angela and I decided to participate in the fun; we needed a mental break too! We started singing the songs he'd written, while he merrily joined in. It was one of the most enjoyable days with him since Martha had died. He finally seemed free of his demons.

A day later, when his condition was stabilized and he came back from that fun-loving place in his mind, he remembered nothing. The only thing he said was, "I'm not afraid to die." I wondered if he had crossed over the line when he was hallucinating and felt the happiness and love on the other side.

He insisted on going home a few days later. I had to get back to California for a business meeting and planned to re-book my Vancouver trip a couple of weeks later. I knew I might not ever see him alive again, but the thought of seeing him continue to suffer was more frightening.

Meanwhile, Angela tried taking Tommy home but once she got there she realized he was completely dependent on the wheelchair. She couldn't lift him up or take care of him. She was forced to call an ambulance to take him back to the hospital, much to his despair. A day later, Vita was admitted to the same hospital with pneumonia. It was if she knew if she weren't inside the hospital, she'd never see him again.

Dear God, thank you for allowing my father to find serenity. Please save him from any long, drawn-out suffering.

Real Life Lesson: You will make your own peace with death when the time comes.

Choices

I'd been in Vancouver for two days when I received several urgent messages from Angela. Tommy had lapsed into a coma and Angela was hysterical because of the violent seizures he was having while unconscious. When I finally got ahold of her at the hospital she was angry with me, screaming I had to get on a plane to New York immediately or I would not see our father alive again.

We left Vancouver the next day for San Francisco. Joe went home and I repacked and left for New York. Having heard Angela describe Tommy's seizures, I was hoping he would be gone before I arrived, for both our sakes. But somehow he held on as if he were waiting to say goodbye to me.

Tommy was in the fifth floor cancer unit and Vita was in the third floor respiratory unit. I went to see Tommy first. Nothing could have prepared me for how he looked. His room was dark and smelled musty, as if a cloud of death was hovering above, just waiting for the right moment to engulf him. He was lying on his side with his eyes open. His body was bloated from the excess body fluids that had started poisoning him as his organs shut down.

I started to cry at the sight of him. When I took his hand in mine and squeezed it tight, I sensed he knew I was there. Occurring at brief intervals, his seizures looked like something out of *The Exorcist*. His face contorted beyond recognition, then his body shook uncontrollably and green bile from his stomach trickled out of his mouth. I prayed to God to take him out of his misery, for he seemed to be in immense pain.

Angela and I alternated floors between Vita and Tommy, keeping Vita abreast of all the details. At some point, I thought how silly we must look, running back and forth between floors, each of us going in a different direction like Laurel and Hardy in a silent movie. I could almost hear the piano music playing in the background as we maneuvered around patients on gurneys, visitors and staff. When we saw each other or Vita, there was no need for words because the drama unfolded via the expressions on our faces. I silently thanked God for helping me find a bit of wacky humor to mix with my solemn thoughts that day.

Vita believed Tommy was going to be okay even though we told her he was dying. She needed to see for herself so, sick as she was, she convinced the nurses on duty to let us take her to see Tommy. We got her into a wheelchair, with a portable IV and oxygen dispenser trailing behind, and headed for the staff elevator. After seven years of frequenting this particular hospital, we no longer considered ourselves visitors.

When she saw him, she tried to wake him up, calling his name over and over again. She told him she loved him and kissed him goodbye. It was the first time I had heard one of them say, "I love you" to the other. Through years of continuous conflict, they'd been a couple who couldn't live with each other and couldn't live without each other.

Shortly after we brought her back to her room, Angela and I saw him take his last breath. The painful expression on his face now vanished as his body stopped shaking and his big, round chest sank slowly down like an accordion on the last note. As we leaned over his body and cried, I imagined him floating above, weightless and serene.

It was one year since he had started chemotherapy and during that time, he had suffered every day. I wondered if he would have gone through it had he known what was to become of his quality of life. Should he have traded one or two good months for twelve painful ones?

Years later, I learned that multiple myeloma patients who undergo chemo usually live one to three years after diagnosis and that only thirty percent make it past five years. I don't know if Tommy ever knew that. If he had, he might've opted to forgo chemotherapy.

I think Tommy gave up on life the day Martha died and it was a broken heart that really killed him. The cancer was his way of checking out, slowly and painfully, as if he were cleansing his soul of the incredible burden of guilt Martha's death had placed upon him.

Dear God, he wasn't supposed to go like this, in such a painful and drawn-out way. He was supposed to slowly drift off into a calm sleep, like they do in the movies. How horrible to have seen the demise of a physical body as it rots away, piece by piece. But I believe he is with you now and that he is without pain and that he does not need that body anymore. Regardless of whether or not he inflicted this disease and suffering upon himself, he did what he felt he needed to do. He fought as he wanted to fight or didn't fight at all. It was his prerogative and I respect it.

Real Life Lesson: While disease may ravage the body, the spirit is eternally in perfect form.

Letting Go

Angela and I decided to keep Tommy's casket closed at the funeral service, despite Vita and Aunt Yolanda's wishes. Vita thought an open casket was the right thing to do and Aunt Yolanda, who had flown in from California, wanted to see her brother one more time. We explained that he now looked like a different person, bald with grayish skin and bloated features. It was not what he would have wanted.

We requested Martha's ashes be put inside his coffin. The mortuary had been holding them for sixteen months and had a difficult time locating them. Even they misfile! They finally found them and placed them inside Tommy's coffin. Vita had been released from the hospital right before the services—as if she could command her body to heal when she needed it to. Go figure!

There was a torrential downpour on the day of the mass and burial, and the rain felt like tears from heaven weeping with us. Angela and I sat in the first row of the church with Vita in her wheelchair right beside us on the aisle. I couldn't believe our family had gone from five to three in little over a year. I'd always expected my family would always be with me. The events—Vita's illness, Martha's suicide, Tommy's cancer and death—had been unimaginable. I remember standing there while the priest was talking and thinking to myself, "Why? What is it all for?" I was angry with God.

The priest started saying something about how God loves us and I remember whispering to Angela, "He's got a hell of a way of showing us!"

Then I became angry with the priest for shaking incense in front of Vita's face, making her gasp for air. Didn't the idiot see her tracheotomy and oxygen tank? I had to wave my hand at him to get him to stop while I wheeled Vita farther away from the pungent fumes.

The days following the funeral were lonely and solemn. Aunt Yolanda had to fly home right after the funeral. One by one, all the visitors left until it was just Vita, Angela and I, with one on-duty nurse and our dog Junior. We knew that once Angela and I left, Vita would be without her family. We didn't want to think about it, so we focused on the various tasks that needed to be done.

I wanted to change the surroundings, erasing any reminder of the way things used to be, so while we cleaned up Tommy's stuff, we moved furniture, got new flooring in the kitchen and cleaned cupboards. This cleansing of the house seemed like a necessary ritual to cleanse our souls of the bad memories and start fresh again.

There was no time to mourn Tommy, because Vita's situation was urgent. She was still alive and still needed us. Her existing insurance would pay for home nursing only if there was another family member living with her. With Tommy gone, the only option was to place her in a nursing home. She was only fifty-seven and still had all her wits about her. We couldn't take her out of her home after all she'd been through.

I knew there had to be a better way. She really didn't need registered nurses. Anyone could learn the procedures, particularly if they were already a nurse's aid or had taken care of a sick relative. Angela, Vita and I decided it was worth spending our own money to keep Vita home. I contacted employment agencies and spent a few weekends interviewing candidates. Many of them didn't drive or speak English. I had to pick some of them up at a bus stop with a big sign telling them who I was. Some worked out, some didn't. But we dealt with problems as they arose. I'm sure Vita always knew that I would fix it!

In addition to Vita's well-being, legal questions concerning the house, debts and wills needed handling. It seemed Tommy thought he was never going to die, since nothing was organized or easy to find. Getting Martha's affairs in order had been just a warm-up for Tommy's.

Vita had no idea where things like mortgage papers, bank statements or credit cards were. We rummaged through Tommy's desk drawers, closets, car and the garage to put the pieces of the puzzle together. It took weeks to figure it all out.

Among his personal items we found copies of the play he had written, which we hadn't read for years. There was also a short story, copies of letters to the editor of various newspapers, and handwritten notes for a story he must have started to write after Vita became ill. The story began with the day he and Vita signed the contract to buy the house and it was obvious from his writing what a huge financial and emotional step this decision represented. He wrote about how much he loved Vita and his children, and how happy he was with his life.

We also found a cassette of Tommy singing his favorite songs. Angela and Martha had coaxed him into making it about ten years earlier. The sound of Tommy's voice, strong and vibrant, brought us all to tears. It was as if he were in the same room with us.

A few weeks later, Angela had a brilliant idea: she took the tape to a small recording studio, where they edited out the background noise and added a piano accompaniment, making it sound like a professional recording. The copies she gave Vita and me were the best gift Tommy could have left us.

On my first trip back to New York after Tommy died, Vita insisted on going with us to choose his tombstone. She spared no expense, choosing a custom-made black marble stone with a picture of a deer engraved near his name and a picture of the Madonna engraved near hers.

She insisted that her name be put on the tombstone with a blank death date. Angela and I thought the idea was morbid but, of course, we didn't go down that route with her! I think it gave her comfort to know she would be with Tommy and Martha when she died.

The memory of Tommy that I keep alive is not the hardened and distant person he became in his last years, or the way he looked and suffered in the end. What I remember about Tommy is the loving, funny, vulnerable side of him that was clearly visible underneath his serious and intimidating exterior. The way he used to sing with a big smile on his face, snapping his fingers to the beat. The way he used to call Vita "Baby Doll" and dance around the kitchen with her. The way he used to suck in his belly to show us he lost weight. The way he used to wheedle out of us what we'd bought him for Christmas. The way he used to sneak into the freezer at night and get ice cream. All these memories captured his true spirit and as the song says, "They can't take that away from me."

God, all this time I kept my faith, thinking you'd come through on this one. Thinking you'd heal Dad since we had suffered so much already, but you didn't. I thought I could influence the outcome with my prayers but I was wrong. I know now that I couldn't change Dad's fate because it was just that: Dad's fate and not mine.

I can't make everything better for everyone. I'm tired of praying and being angry with you and my family when things don't turn out perfectly. I just hope now that Ma will be able to live at home with all the help she needs.

Dad, I'm picturing you right now—the old you. You're with Grandma, sitting on a great big comfortable chair eating a big plate of spaghetti with a bowl of ice cream waiting in the wings. After you eat, you and Grandma will sing all those Italian songs you used to sing. I hope you're happy now. I know you did your best in life as a husband and father. Don't worry about Ma. She'll be okay; she's a survivor. I long to hear your voice, even a big angry yell! I love you, Dad.

Real Life Lesson: It's okay to be angry when your prayers are not answered, but it's wise to accept what you cannot control.

Real Life Lessons
from Tommy

Having spent a lot more time with Vita than with Tommy when I was growing up, I'd say I learned more from her. She taught me all the domestic and social skills I needed to become a considerate, well-liked, well-groomed person. Tommy seemed to be more concerned about teaching us what we shouldn't do rather than what we should do. Looking back, though, I realize he taught me a great deal about what was important in life.

When I was seven years old, I got my first two-wheeler bike. It was cobalt blue with a pink banana seat, monkey handlebars and a white plastic basket decorated with colorful flowers. I didn't know how to ride yet, but I was determined to be just as good as Angela, who had been riding a two-wheeler for a couple of years. On the first day, I repeatedly tried to balance on two wheels, but couldn't. I gave up and despondently wheeled my prize possession into the garage.

I ran into the house crying, "I can't do it! I can't do it! I don't want to ride anymore!" That would be the first of many times I would hear my father say, "Don't ever say you can't, because you can do anything you put your mind to."

The next day he bought me a set of training wheels and within a week, I didn't need them. Over the years, whenever I felt like I was in a situation I couldn't conquer, I would remind myself of his words. I knew I could accomplish anything as long as I didn't give up. Perseverance and positive thinking will always prevail in my life. These values not only helped me in my professional life, but in my personal life as well, particularly in dealing with Vita's life-and-death challenges.

Real Life Lesson: If you say you can, you will.

Another poignant lesson came much later in my life, when Tommy was undergoing chemotherapy. I had been promoted to associate publisher of a magazine, which was the equivalent of being vice-president of a small company and included a considerable jump in status and compensation. I couldn't wait to tell Tommy on my next visit to New York, since he had always been impressed with my earning power in the corporate market.

Tommy used to boast to his friends about his highly successful, college graduate daughter. It was a world apart from the union environment and pay to which he was accustomed, although he never understood exactly what I did and why it seemed like I had to work twenty-four hours a day. On this occasion, however, when I shared my news with him, his reaction was different.

After an unemotional word of congratulations, he asked, "Debbie, how much money do you need?"

I didn't know how to respond. I had never really thought about it. I was a young, ambitious businesswoman with a fast-track career. The most important objectives at work (a.k.a. my life) were status and money. His one simple question put everything into perspective.

There's a touching scene at the end of *It's a Wonderful Life*, when all the townspeople come to the rescue of poor George Bailey. One at a time they enter his home, smiling ear-to-ear, with words of thanks as they empty their meager savings into a big basket. In the final moments of the movie,

George's brother lifts his glass and toasts him for being the richest man in town. That's my cue to get the tissues!

The accumulation of money is not what makes a person rich. Richness and fulfillment only come from the accumulation of love and respect from your fellow human beings.

Real Life Lesson: Life is not about the money you have but about the people you touch.

Another lesson I learned didn't come from a conversation or a specific incident. It was a lesson by example. It was about a quality in my father that existed in him throughout his life. It was about integrity and the moral and ethical strength he possessed that manifested itself in true honesty.

Integrity is the foundation I strive to build my life upon, realizing that the moment I allow it to splinter, I lose the very core of myself. It is the one thing that makes me whole no matter what situation I face, what decision I make or how others may judge me.

Real Life Lesson: Be true to yourself and others, and you'll know the difference between right and wrong.

Among Tommy's personal writings, we found a letter to the editor of the local newspaper, which was published in 1975. I don't know what provoked his thoughts but it surely reflected his true character. It was entitled "Moral Obligations."

In pondering all the confusion existing in the world today, one wonders just how and why it evolved to such cataclysm. Have we lost sight of the fundamental principle of humanity? Why do we refuse to adhere to our inner conscience in our daily existence? Or—God help us—have we lost our conscience, too?

We have heard man justify his ill deeds by stating, "In the long run, I did more good than bad." Certainly, this is the pinnacle of absurdity, a warped sense of justification. And yet it seems the premise of our society. This unrelenting dogma—if you will—ultimately will destroy us!

MAN—in any field of endeavor—whether he has the responsibility of the masses, or of his next-door neighbor only, must realize that to hurt one is to hurt all. For we were created equal. Unfortunately, many times it takes a tragic event to awaken man to his wrongdoing.

When will we ever discover what wonderful fruits we can reap, individually and collectively, if only we adhere to our moral obligation to God and man.

Wake up, brothers and sisters, soon it may be too late!

Thomas Gisonni

I keep these memories of my father close to my heart and try to apply them in my actions. Tommy didn't teach me as many lessons as Vita did. He just taught me some of the biggest ones.

Real Life Lesson: Just because someone may not consider his own life a success doesn't mean he has nothing to teach you.

Tommy in one of his many fedoras
1990

IV

YOLANDA

Yo's Turn

After Tommy died, I poured myself into work once again. The demands of my job in the high stress high-tech industry increased with each promotion I received. However, work also meant I traveled east a great deal more than I had before, which allowed me to visit Vita more frequently. Much of my spare time in California and all of it in New York was devoted to making sure her at-home care was on track, and handling any other specific needs she had. Although I had lived in California for six years, I still referred to New York as home.

There were only a few close friends at work who knew what had happened to Martha and Tommy, or that my mother had been sick for so many years. I couldn't subject colleagues to the constant ups and downs of my emotions or even the bare outline of my family saga. I needed to stay focused on my job, to which I felt enormous loyalty and commitment. Regardless of what was going on in my personal life, I was determined to excel at work and I did.

Since moving to California, I had grown very close to Aunt Yolanda, or Aunt Yo, as I called her. She was like a second mother to me. The strong attachment between us had started the day I was born. A few years before, Aunt Yo had given birth to a stillborn baby girl who was to have been named Deborah. Vita liked the name so much that she gave it to me.

Growing up, I was constantly told how much I was like Aunt Yolanda. I had her dark eyes and complexion, black curly hair, tenacious personality and love of sweets. My only physical resemblance to Vita was my petite frame.

Until I was four years old, Aunt Yo, Uncle Joe and their three sons lived in the same three-story Bronx apartment building we did. We occupied the ground floor and they lived above us. Grandpa and Grandma Gisonni had the third floor. Once Aunt Yo and Uncle Joe moved to California, we rarely saw them, although Aunt Yo and I kept in touch by writing letters.

When I was in college, she invited me to take a cruise with her. Since there was such a strong resemblance, everyone assumed we were mother and daughter and she loved passing me off as her own. Naturally, when she heard about my opportunity in California, she was delighted and invited me to stay with her and Uncle Joe until I was settled. Her boys had moved away from home by then.

Living with Aunt Yo gave me a chance to really get to know her as an adult. I felt as comfortable in her house as I would have in my own; she was family, after all. The environment was calming after the turmoil I left behind in New York and it reminded me how life had been before Vita got sick. I stayed there six months, until I found my own apartment, only twenty minutes away.

We spent holidays together, saw each other or at least talked several times a week, and frequently spent Sunday afternoons shopping at the local malls. She spent Saturday cleaning her house and cooking several meals for the week. I would go by and chat with her while she fed me samples of whatever was ready. She told me stories from her childhood, growing up with Tommy, which gave me new insight into my father.

Like Tommy, she had a hard childhood on the family farm. I remember her telling me how she used to spend hours and hours picking the bugs off the potatoes! After high school, she learned bookkeeping (when all of that was done by hand!) and got married quite young—probably to get out of the house and away from her father. Although she had a strong work ethic, like Tommy, she hated her job. I don't know what Yo's dreams where in life but I do know that she felt she deserved not to have to struggle so much.

When Joe left New York to be with me in California, Aunt Yo immediately adopted him as her favorite nephew. She relied on him, as Vita had done, to fix anything and everything that needed fixing around the house. Joe was a handy man's handy man, always willing and ready to help out when needed.

Aunt Yo and Vita, although close in age, were worlds apart in their thinking. Maybe it was the difference between being an aunt and being a mother. While mothers can be excessively judgmental, aunts never are. Vita was my mother, not my friend. There was a strict line that I never crossed. But with Yo, I could cross that line and still respect her. Because my relationship with her developed when I moved to California in my early twenties, she always treated me like an adult. We never fought with each other. We were both just so happy to be around each other. Me, because her company was so soothing after the chaos I'd left behind; and her, because I was the daughter she'd always wanted—without her having to go through the hassle of raising me!

Aunt Yo said to me, "Don't waste your money on a big wedding, just to make everyone else happy. If you don't want that, just elope." Vita had her book of rules on that particular subject and engraved in stone was the necessity of a huge traditional Italian wedding in some fancy wedding hall with too much food for a multitude of guests you didn't even know! For a short while—about a minute—Joe and I considered doing "the right thing" (according to Vita), but it would have been difficult enough to plan it three thousand miles away, even without her volatile health, which could land her in the hospital at any moment.

Joe and I opted to break the rules and elope on Valentine's Day, 1988. It was a sore spot with Vita until the day she died. Vita didn't speak to me for two months after I got married. I still called her every day and sent her my good wishes through her nurse. I figured she'd come around eventually and on Easter Sunday, she did. She probably had another rule about not staying mad at your daughter past a religious holiday. She got on the phone that day and talked to me as if nothing had happened. Of course, she never missed an opportunity to tell me how disappointed she was that I hadn't been married in a Catholic Church, in the eyes of God.

In the months following Tommy's death, Aunt Yo became a bit withdrawn. I didn't talk to her as much and she didn't seem to be her usual self. I just assumed she was grieving for her brother in her own way and needed her own space. While that may have been true, it wasn't the main reason. I didn't know she had discovered a lump in her breast and was awaiting the biopsy results before alarming me with any news. Given what I had just gone through with Tommy, she didn't want to burden me. When the results came in, she called to tell me she had breast cancer.

This time, the word *cancer* hit a much different chord than it had a year before when Tommy got it. Then, it was still the unknown but treatable thing. The thing you could talk about without any emotion, that one-half of all Americans got. That's all it'd meant to me the year before. But now, the word *cancer* was a deep wound, scarred but still sensitive to the touch. I knew this word all too well. I knew how powerful it was. I knew all the small battles Aunt Yo would have to fight and the war she would eventually have to win. It sent chills up my spine and I could barely spit out any words of encouragement. Aunt Yo and Dad—both of them getting cancer. Was this what I had to look forward to in my old age? It was a scary thought.

She was scheduled to have a mastectomy, which would be followed by a six-month chemotherapy program. The survival statistics for breast cancer were much better than for multiple myeloma: over eighty percent of those diagnosed were still living five years later. There was hope.

She came through the operation fine. They removed one breast and a number of infected lymph nodes. Chemotherapy started immediately. Fortunately, Aunt Yo's chemotherapy was not as debilitating as Tommy's, which was a promising sign. All cancers are not alike, I thought. Aunt Yo could make it through this. She even continued to work through most of it and complained very little.

Since my move to California, I had been Aunt Yo's niece from New York, almost a surrogate daughter. But now, I fully assumed the role of daughter, with the same dialogue and gestures I knew so well from the last seven years with Vita. I visited more often, cooked and cleaned for her, took care of her and helped in whatever way necessary. I didn't think about it; I just did it. Vita naturally approved of and encouraged this behavior. After all, this was the kind of person she had raised me to be. Aunt Yo's boys were all a plane ride away and could not help on a daily basis. There was a reason I had come to California and this was apparently it.

Dear God, I feel numb again from this latest news. It never gets any easier, just more familiar. It feels like everyone I love is slipping through my fingers under a sea of black water, as I desperately try to hold onto them. Is it a lost cause? Is it another scare to test me, to test us? To help us get our faith back? Is it a way to show her how Dad suffered?

I pray for Aunt Yo. I pray that anyone who loves her, dead or alive, prays for her. I beg you to spare her life. I need to keep her in mine.

Real Life Lesson: Sometimes, a road you choose in life has already been chosen, whether or not you recognize it at the time.

Darling, You Look Marvelous!

Remember the suavely comic impersonation Billy Crystal did of Fernando Lamas on *Saturday Night Live?* The trademark line, delivered in a very romantic Latin accent—"Dahling, you look maaavelous"—became part of American pop culture. I never would have dreamt that silly saying would mean so much to me when Vita and Yolanda were sick.

For as long as I can remember, Vita was always perfectly "done." Her coiffed, heavily sprayed hair never moved an inch and her red lipstick stayed on all day—a feat I am still not able to equal. When most of my teenage friends' mothers were in elastic waist pants, Vita, with her petite frame and young looks, was sporting trendy designer jeans.

Aunt Yo had the same notions about appearance. Her fashionable clothes came with matching shoes and handbag. She loved jewelry and had a lot of it. Her flawlessly smooth olive skin only required a bit of blush, lipstick and mascara to bring out her classic beauty. I remember watching her apply mascara and then painstakingly separate each lash with a toothpick to get them looking just right. Yolanda and Vita's biggest role models were Sophia Loren and Jackie Kennedy. Sophia, with her full lips and swinging hips, was their Italian connection. Jackie, with her impeccable style and manners, was their American princess.

Vita and Yolanda imparted this sense of style to their children. Although money was tight, we always looked neat and fashionable. Vita made sure of it. Even as we grew to adulthood, she would take it upon herself to comment on our appearance. It was like listening to Joan Rivers do her celebrity bashing, only with an Italian accent.

"Put on some lipstick, you looka dead," Vita would say or, "Don't wear those buggy (her word for *baggy*) pants, they make you looka fat." Although a therapist might say such cruel and unusual comments caused irreparable emotional damage, I don't think it was bad for us. We knew it was just Vita's way. To this day, I feel obliged to fix my hair and face every day, even if I'm not going anywhere.

When they were sick, Vita and Aunt Yo never lost their commitment to look their best. Vita learned to use her left hand to perform daily rituals. She combed her hair and applied make-up every morning, except when immobilized on a respirator. Due to her physical condition, her wardrobe was limited. Pants needed elastic waists for easy removal and tops needed V-neck collars for access to her tracheotomy opening.

She would employ nurses or friends to convert regular shirt collars into V-necks, giving her more wardrobe choices. People always told her how great she looked despite her illness, and it made her feel like a million bucks to hear those compliments. She would often say something like, "Aunt Mary couldn't get over how good I looka, and could you believa, I'm in so much pain!"

What bothered Aunt Yo most about the many side effects of chemotherapy was the change in her physical appearance. She lost all of her hair. I remember the day she said she woke up with no eyelashes. This immediately sent her running to the drugstore for false ones, as she was not about to be seen in public without eyelashes! She kept her Wednesday hair appointment, just as she had for thirty years, only her stylist worked on her wig instead of her head!

Saturday was the one day of the week Aunt Yo indulged herself, which for her meant a long hot bath followed by polishing her nails. Her new morning routine during the week included fixing her wig perfectly on her bald head, applying false eyelashes along with her make-up and inserting a fake breast she called her "falsie" into her bra before going off to work. When she left the house, she looked stunning! No one would have guessed what she was going through.

Vita and Yolanda's commitment to looking good while they were feeling bad taught me how important it is to treat yourself with respect no matter what happens to your body. You cannot love others without first loving yourself. To Vita and Aunt Yo, this meant creating a beautiful appearance. Wouldn't it be grand if all hospitals provided free hair, make-up and decorating services from visiting professionals?

Real Life Lesson: True beauty comes from within, but a little blush and lipstick don't hurt either.

California, Here They Come

After six months of chemotherapy, Aunt Yo was on the road to recovery. She was still abnormally tired, but extremely happy that her blood work showed no sign of cancer. In the meantime, I had convinced Vita to come out to visit us. Up until this point, a trip to the local mall or Long Island to visit her sister was as far as she had gotten during the eight years since her surgery.

Most people would never have considered sending a person in Vita's condition on a plane for a six-hour trip across the country. Vita herself didn't believe she could do it. I knew it would be difficult to arrange, but I focused on the steps necessary to get it done, because it was the one thing I knew would give her great pleasure.

I called the airline's medical advisors, got letters from her doctors, arranged to have two people come with her, ordered every medical supply that she regularly used, and rented a hospital bed, an oxygen tank, and a bed tray. I even packed her suitcase for her while I was in New York on business. Then I prayed she wouldn't get sick and have to cancel.

In July 1992, Vita boarded a flight with her friend and nurse Pat Foyder, her live-in aide Regina, and all her portable medical machines.

When they arrived in San Francisco, she was the last one to be taken off the plane. I got anxious waiting for her, hoping she wasn't having a seizure,

121

but when they finally wheeled her off, she looked beautiful. Her make-up and hair were intact, as usual, and her clothing was carefully chosen for comfort, style and color. After all those years of pseudo-imprisonment, she was finally on vacation! I was determined to make it the best ten days of her life.

We took her medical supplies and wheelchair with us everywhere we went in the Bay Area. I wheeled her up the hills of San Francisco and around the shops in Sausalito. We ate at restaurants every day (something she hadn't done for years) and drank piña coladas every night. I even threw a barbecue in her honor with Aunt Yo and all my friends.

I took pictures of everything we did: all of us waving in front of the entrance to Chinatown, Aunt Yo and Vita relaxing at Aunt Yo's house, even Vita cutting up tomatoes for a salad. I had four sets of pictures printed and organized Vita's into a mini-album. I wanted to save those memories forever. She was the happiest I had seen her in years. My only regret was that Tommy wasn't there to enjoy it with her.

On second thought, maybe it was better he wasn't there. He would've had to fight his way into the one bathroom that four women seemed to occupy at the same time! Joe gave up his rights to it and showered at work that week. There's something about wearing open hospital gowns, or being around people who do, that eventually eliminates any need for normal privacy. All delicacy gets flushed down the toilet and the bathroom becomes a group activities room.

Despite the deaths and illness that had recently plagued her, there was this one week where Vita's medical condition didn't set the agenda. The photos radiate intensely positive energy, as if you could feel the happiness. Pictures of Vita coming off the plane and standing in front of the Golden Gate Bridge show her looking totally happy.

After she returned to New York, Vita kept that photo album on the coffee table and showed it to everyone who came by. She had finally made it out to California to see her Debbie and her sister-in-law, and she was damn proud of herself! So many of her friends told me that she couldn't stop talking about her trip. It gave her so much pleasure and that made my heart sing!

Dear God, I'm so happy right now. Aunt Yo is doing fine and Ma actually made it out here. I loved being with the two of them together. It's such a strong bond I have with them—like two mothers. Thank you, Lord, for making this possible. For giving Ma a few days of fun, away from her misery. Thank you for letting Aunt Yo get through her pain quickly.

Real Life Lesson: You don't have to solve all of someone's problems to bring joy into their life.

The Other Side

About a month after Vita returned to New York, she left a message on my answering machine—a tell-tale sign something was wrong. First, she never left phone messages; she had a phobia about that. Second, she rarely called me. The rules were pretty explicit in that area. The daughter is supposed to call the mother at all times, out of respect, of course.

I got a chuckle listening to her raspy voice on my answering machine for the first time. "Debbie—Debbie, are you there?" Wouldn't I have answered if I were? Okay, maybe I wouldn't have. "It's Mommy." As if I couldn't tell. "Something is wrong with Junior! I don't know what to do."

Junior was fifteen years old by then. I knew her days were numbered but was unprepared to let go of her. I called Vita back immediately. Vita said Junior was walking into walls and furniture, but that's not what bothered her. The fact that Junior wasn't eating was to her a more serious symptom.

Since the dog was not the responsibility of the in-home aides and nurses, Vita had called me. Naturally, she assumed I could figure it out three thousand miles away! I had a feeling she was afraid that Junior would have to be put down, and she didn't want to make that decision without my knowing. Junior and all the other dogs we ever had were unofficially mine to take care of. I was the animal lover in the family.

I told Vita to call Pat, whose daughter had found and brought us Junior. Pat took Junior to the vet and was told the situation was serious. Junior had suffered a stroke and brain damage. She wouldn't recover. Putting her to sleep was the only humane thing to do. Another family loss.

Junior's death was heavy with symbolism. She was the last connection to Vita's home life to be taken away. I felt deeply guilty about the whole situation, as if I had abandoned Junior in her time of need. After I moved to California, Martha had taken care of Junior. After Martha's death, Junior was left to her own devices. She was fed and let out, but Vita and Tommy were too consumed with their own problems to pay much attention to her.

I wondered where Junior would go when she died. From my Catholic upbringing, I believed that a person's soul lives on beyond the death of the physical body, but what about pets? James Van Praagh's *Talking to Heaven* was not out yet, but when I read the psychic channeler's book years later, it all made perfect sense. Van Praagh says that both humans and animals pass over from one vibrational frequency to another when they die. They go to a place where time and distance are irrelevant, and pain and suffering nonexistent. His belief, based on conversations with people and their deceased loved ones, sounds like something Saint Augustine said: "Death is nothing. I've just passed into another room. Dry your tears if you love me."

I'd been drying my tears for years now and wanted to believe that Martha, Tommy and Junior were still close to me, as if in another room. Many stories from people who have had near-death experiences support this theory. I don't know how Vita or Tommy would react to Van Praagh's explanation, but I do know that they believed in life after death. They referred to dead relatives as being "on the other side," which kept their connection to their families alive, and gave them hope that they would eventually be reunited.

They talked to them or about them as if they were in another city. "Grandma Gisonni must be enjoying a big bowl of macaroni right now,"

Tommy would say. Vita often thought she saw her mother sitting on the chair by her bed in the evenings, as if she were watching over her while she was sick. She would have entire conversations with her that gave her a sense of peace and comfort. They didn't need any proof that this afterlife existed. They just believed it did. And so did I.

After Junior was put to sleep Vita said, "I bet your sister Martha is taking Junior for a long walk right now."

"I'm sure she is!"

After Junior died, I said a special prayer to her.

Junior, I remember the first day you came into our family with your sweet breath and pink belly. It was Thanksgiving weekend and we fed you turkey. You looked like a little black fur ball and you loved falling asleep on Dad's big chest! You were such a good little dog, performing tricks for treats, giving us such joy for so many years. I remember how excited you'd get when I took your leash out. I used to love to walk you down to the schoolyard to play and run around.

I can't imagine what you thought about all that happened in the house these last few years. First I left, then Martha and then Dad. Junior, I hope your last days here were not painful and that you're somewhere with Martha and Dad right now. Thanks for everything you've given us. I'll miss you and so will Vita.

Real Life Lesson: Think of lost loved ones as being in another room, and they will never die in your heart.

The Blackout

By fall 1993, Aunt Yo's hair had grown back a beautiful silver color and she'd decided not to dye it black anymore. Her chemo treatments had been over for months but she was more tired than ever. She had constant pain under her arm where lymph nodes had been removed, and her hands were frequently swollen and stiff.

She'd received a saline-type breast implant, due to a temporary moratorium on silicone. No matter what they did to this new breast, it didn't look anything like her other one. She felt deformed and embarrassed, but she was part of a generation who kept silent about such things. The only indication she ever gave of how she felt was one night when we were alone. "Look at this body," she said. "Who would want to go to bed with this?"

It was a surprising thing for her to say to me. Caught off guard, I didn't know what to say, so I just changed the subject. Unfortunately, breast cancer was for her, as for so many women, an attack on her femininity, destroying the part of her that defined her womanhood. Understandably, Aunt Yo was not comfortable talking to outsiders about such an intimate problem. She refused to see a counselor or join a support group. She wanted to handle it on her own.

One night, Aunt Yo called to tell me she'd been in an accident driving to work and totaled her car. She'd apparently blacked out behind the wheel and woken up in a hospital emergency room. Luckily, she sustained only minor cuts and bruises. When they conducted some tests, however, they discovered multiple secondary lumps around her breast. She would need a more aggressive treatment this time, consisting of high doses of radiation.

When she had her mastectomy, there'd been one doctor who suggested radiation in addition to chemotherapy, because of the large number of infected lymph nodes, but his impersonal manner pissed off Aunt Yo, who was not ready to be handed a death sentence. She'd listened instead to another doctor with a brighter outlook, who recommended chemo only. I wondered if that would have made a difference. We'd never know. Aunt Yo started the radiation treatments and became weaker and weaker.

The first weekend after radiation, I volunteered to stay with her at her house. I hadn't seen her since the accident and when I did, my heart sank. I had seen that same face before: the hollowed-out eyes and the yellow-green complexion. It was Tommy's face before he died. It was the face of death. It was the face of a body being ravaged from the inside out. I knew the fight was over. Aunt Yo had been defeated. It made me sick to my stomach.

How could this have happened to such a strong woman? She grew up tough as nails, surviving a childhood with four brothers and an abusive father. She was able to hold her own with the best of them, verbally and physically. Why couldn't she fight this and be one of the survivors? How could she let this beat her? No one had ever messed with Aunt Yo until now. Until her fate seemed to be taken over by a higher power. I had already learned to accept what could not be changed. I put on my happy face and cooked up a storm of meals for the week ahead.

When I came home, I called Angela and said, "Aunt Yo is going to die soon."

"What do you mean? I thought they were going to be able to treat her."

I said, "They are, but it won't help. Believe me. I know."

God, I'm not going to plead. I'm only going to accept your will as reality.
What will be, will be. But please take her quickly and painlessly.

Real Life Lesson: Real strength is sometimes the acceptance of unavoidable loss.

Another Ending

Aunt Yo continued radiation treatments in the weeks that followed. Her condition seemed to get worse and her chest looked as if it had been burned in a fire. I brought food to her and Uncle Joe almost every day. Food—it's what we Italians live for—the fix-all and ultimate comfort. During this time, however, I learned about another remedy, one without calories: the healing power of touch.

While I didn't think anything would cure Aunt Yo, I wanted to do whatever I could to make her comfortable and happy. I had learned from Vita's experience how difficult it could be for people, even family members, to touch someone who doesn't look well. But for the sick or dying, human touch is irreplaceable.

Whenever I visited Aunt Yo, after I applied burn cream to her blisters, I would spend hours rubbing lotion on her arms, hands, legs, feet and back while she lay in bed. She was so grateful and always thanked me again and again before I left. I was glad I could give her this comfort.

Within a month, the doctors informed us that the cancer had spread to Aunt Yo's liver. I was not surprised. They attempted more treatment, but it didn't help. They gave her three to six months to live. She lasted less than two.

Her family decided not to tell her she was dying. They couldn't bear to break her heart. I'm not sure that was the best decision, but it wasn't mine to make. I felt it was unfair to her, as she might have wanted to say her goodbyes. I cancelled all my business travel over the next few weeks. She was readmitted to the hospital, but still thought she was going to recover.

After a week in the hospital, she started going in and out of consciousness. She was on morphine to relieve the pain. I had postponed my business trips as much as possible, but I had to go to New York to give year-end presentations to the board of directors. The night before I left, I visited her in her hospital room. I nearly gagged on the rancid smell of death. It reminded me of Tommy's room before he died. She started talking about Vita.

"I don't know how your mother endured all of this for so many years. The sickness, the disability and dependence on others, on top of Martha and my brother dying. And yet, she still fights. I gotta give her credit. I've only gone through a drop in the bucket compared to her and I don't think I can take it anymore."

Vita and Aunt Yolanda, two very strong-willed women, both of them crippled with illness. One was going to die after a few months of suffering and the other had nine lives and nine years of pain. I'm not sure who got the short end of the stick.

When it came time to say goodbye, I knew it was the last time I would see her alive. I started to cry and she said, "Why are you crying? What's wrong?" She really didn't know.

The phone call came two days after I arrived in New York. Joe tracked me down at work and told me. I finished my presentations to the board and then went to Vita's. I decided not to fly back for the funeral. I had done everything I could for Aunt Yo in her last days. There was nothing I could do for her now. It was more important for me to focus on Vita. She was alone.

Dear God, thank you for ending Aunt Yo's suffering quickly. I loved her like my own mother and I'm grateful that I had the opportunity to be with her and get to know her in California. It's funny how things happen.

Aunt Yo, I hope that I was able to give you what you always wanted in a daughter. You'll always be in my heart and every time I look in the mirror, I'm reminded of some part of you that is also a part of me. Saturday afternoons won't be the same without you.

Real Life Lesson: Even when someone is dying, there's much you can do to comfort them.

Yolanda, Vita and Debbie (L-R)
Vita's trip to California
1992

V

YEAR TEN

Vita's Will

I once read somewhere that it's not the spirit that occupies the body, but the body that occupies the spirit. The spirit prevails, even when the body is failing. Vita was a great example of this. She wasn't expected to live nine years after her operation, but she did. The doctors said she would never get off a respirator, but she did. They said she would never walk again, but she did. They said she would never eat again, but she did. They said she would never be able to live at home, but she did. She repeatedly beat the odds.

Because of her spirit, Vita consistently rose above the physical and emotional indignities of her illness. Her will to live was an extension of her everyday willfulness. Her persistent, controlling nature never wavered during her illness, never mellowed. If anything, she became more demanding and inflexible.

As a child in Italy, Vita had survived the horrors of World War II. Later in life, she faced another war. A war between her will and her body. She pushed herself to gain the slightest advances in that war. Nothing forced her to retreat, not even the death of her husband and daughter. She managed to survive, believing they were in a better place than she was, and paid homage to them by wearing black for months after they died.

Vita was dependent on others for virtually all her physical needs. She who had cared for her own and other people's babies was now taken care of like a baby. She could no longer get up and walk, roll over in bed, or attend to her personal needs. The hands that used to work as fast as a machine were almost useless. Her body that was once petite, curvy and healthy had become frail and hunched over with osteoporosis and muscular atrophy. She had to take over fifty pills a day, for all the secondary ailments that surfaced over the years after the operation.

Food, which once defined her existence as an Italian mother, became a scientific experiment that could kill her if it didn't go down the right way. For the first three years after her operation, she could not taste food, even as she smelled the aroma of what others were eating. All of this seemed unreal. It was as if she had enrolled in a Ph.D. in suffering and was committed to finishing with top honors!

When Vita talked about her pre-illness days, she'd start off by saying, "When I was alive—" Then she'd realize her mistake and say, "I mean, before my operation—" She didn't have to correct herself. We knew exactly what she meant: many physical parts of her were as good as dead. Her spirit, however, was as alive as ever.

Vita's consistency fueled her iron will. She kept all of her daily rituals, routines and beliefs intact. Every morning she religiously did her make-up and hair at the kitchen table with her nurse's assistance. Then she would say her rosary, with the beads that Martha and I had brought back from the Vatican. After that, the radio was turned on for local news and music. While she listened, she performed vocal exercises not unlike the ones actors do. Then came breakfast.

During the day, television was both her link to the outside world and a temporary distraction from her own life. *All My Children* or "My Story" as she referred to it, came on at one o'clock. She could get lost in a place where love, betrayal, friendship, childbirth, death, murder, drugs and comas were all squeezed into one dramatic hour of TV. Later in the afternoon came *Oprah*, her favorite show of the day. She loved hearing the stories of conflict and triumph in other people's lives. At six and eleven, she watched the news, just as she had done with Tommy for as long as I could remember.

In between television shows, Vita indulged her passion for cooking. Even without sharp motor skills in her hands, she managed to cut, chop and mold foods. It took her a lot longer and she looked like an awkward kid with a knife in her hands for the first time, but she managed. She would ask the nurses to bring her the pot from the stove to the kitchen table where she was sitting so she could check on it. I bought her an electric frying pan so she could cook certain foods right there on the table. She would peel garlic by banging the cloves with a pot to loosen the skin. She always had something special for me when I came to visit. Despite all that had happened, she still derived great pleasure from cooking and feeding people.

Every Sunday morning at ten she anxiously awaited the arrival of Jack, a deacon from the local Catholic Church. He came with a "travel light" version of the mass complete with candles, holy water, 3x5 picture of Christ on the cross, bible and communion wafer. He set up his altar on Vita's kitchen table, then proceeded to read from the scriptures, recite prayers and administer communion. The nurses who weren't Jewish usually participated in the ceremony and at the end, they all joined hands for the Lord's prayer.

Vita wanted me to sit in on the mass whenever I visited her, but I wasn't comfortable with it. I was never a joiner. I didn't need organized religion to pray, particularly since I no longer agreed with many of the beliefs of the Catholic Church. I prayed in my own way, privately, creating my own personal link to God and the universe. Vita could never understand my feelings about it, so I used to duck into the shower just before communion.

I was glad to chat with Jack after the ceremony was over. That's when the coffee and cake was served, for the social part of his visit. Vita would ask if her name had been mentioned in church that week and Jack would confirm that it had. It was her fifteen minutes of fame. Jack became quite a friend to her and our family over the years. Vita really loved him. After he left, she would turn the TV back on and watch the Italian station that aired every Sunday afternoon in New York.

The only departure from this stable world she created at home was when she developed pneumonia, which sent her back to the hospital. She always fought it, knowing that each time she left her house could be the last time. She didn't want to die.

I think she actually did die once during a hospital stay, but came right back to life. What people call an out-of-body experience. Angela and I were visiting her; she was extremely weak. With limited lung capacity, it was very difficult for her to expel the excess mucous that built up in her lungs during the infection. It took a tremendous amount of energy to cough these fluids up through her trachea opening. All of a sudden, her face muscles contorted into a gruesome, pain-filled expression. She couldn't speak and her eyes started rolling back. Thick mucous had plugged her airway and she couldn't breathe.

We ran for help and the nurses called a "code blue" over the intercom, immediately summoning as much help as possible. About ten minutes later, they had cleared the plug and revived her. Right afterwards, Vita said, "Can you ask the doctor for a copy of that videotape?"

"What tape? What do you mean?" I asked.

"The tape I was just watching on TV, with the doctors working on me."

I told her there was no such tape, that she must have been dreaming. She insisted I speak to the doctor. I knew there was no tape, but in order to humor her and keep her calm, I walked out of the room to "speak to the doctor." I came back and told her there was no tape. She didn't believe me and proceeded to tell me what she had seen, which matched exactly what had happened in the room a few minutes earlier while she was unconscious.

One explanation was that she'd seen them trying to revive her, but that didn't fit because she saw it all from above, as if she were watching herself in a movie. I was sure she had had an out-of-body, near-death experience. I tried to explain this to her but she couldn't understand. She just kept insisting vehemently that there was a videotape of this whole incident and we were hiding it from her.

She came home from that hospital stay, just as she always had, and it wasn't long before she was wearing her red lipstick again. She *was* the color red: the color of vibrant passion, power and energy.

Dear God, thank you for giving Vita the strength to survive all these years and the will to be with us and continue giving us the gifts of her character and her spirit. At times she drives me crazy, but she never stops amazing me with her perseverance. It puts any little complaint I could ever have in perspective. How does she do it, day after day?

Real Life Lesson: The strength of your will is the greatest force for healing both body and soul.

Somehow You Know

In April 1994, Vita had another pneumonia relapse, which landed her in the hospital for a month. Afterwards, she was so weak that the doctors sent her to the same rehabilitation facility she had been in years before. She was supposed to stay there from one to three months.

In the rehab center, Vita's spirits revived. She loved her aqua-therapy class and how light she felt in the pool, although she had never learned to swim. The water took away all the stress and heaviness of her body. Then one day on the phone, she sounded depressed. She was congested. She and I both knew the danger in that. We had been there so many times before. She was on the verge of pneumonia again. The next day, she was sent back into the ICU.

I had just been made publisher of a magazine: the highest position I'd held so far in the corporate world—like being president of a company within a company. I came to New York for business meetings. The day before I saw Vita, Jackie Onassis died. They were the same age. I knew Vita would want to know the news, but I had another reason for wanting to tell her. I wanted her to know that it was okay to let go, that it happens to all of us, even the famous and the beautiful. I feared her death but I also feared her going on living like this.

After my visit, when I got up to leave, I fixed everything around her just as I had done for the last ten years: I pulled the tray close to her bed, filled the water pitcher, and arranged her tissues and buzzer so that they were within arm's reach. She still wanted things exactly the way she wanted them. I kissed her goodbye as usual and started to walk down the hallway. I felt as tired and weary as she looked. Tired of the treks across the country. Tired of seeing her sick. Tired of managing her care. Tired of cheering her on. Tired of all of it. All of a sudden, I was overwhelmed with sadness and started to cry. I rarely cried when I left her, but something was different that night.

One week later, her primary doctor called me in California. Vita was still in the ICU and I figured he needed approval for something and hadn't been able to reach Angela.

"Debbie," he said, "something happened to your mother. She had a heart seizure."

That figures, I thought. One more crisis to deal with. "Is she going to be okay?"

He paused, realizing I didn't understand. After all, why should I? Vita was the Rock of Gibraltar, the unsinkable Molly Brown, the lioness with more than nine lives. She had been to hell and back so many times, why would this be any different?

"I mean her heart stopped. She's gone."

At that moment, I think my own heart stopped.

"Oh, my God, I can't believe it," I blurted out. And I really couldn't. I didn't think anything could beat her. Heart trouble was the one thing that didn't concern us because the doctors always said she had a strong heart. Who would have guessed her heart would finally stop supporting her failing body? Vita's will finally lost against the elements. She had come to the end of her journey. It was exactly ten years to the month of her operation, when we'd assumed the only interruption in our family and our lives would be her six-week hospital stay.

I hung up the phone, dialed Angela while I was still able to talk and left her an urgent message. Then I started frantically pacing around my house, yelling and screaming and crying all at the same time. "Oh, my God! Oh, my God! I can't believe she's gone. That's it. I'll never see her again. Oh, my God! she's gone. After all this, she dies alone. Oh, my God. I can't fucking believe this."

I finally landed on the floor in my kitchen, crying hysterically, with my two ten-week-old puppies huddled around me, wondering what was wrong. Joe wasn't due home for another hour or so. Later, I said a prayer to Vita.

Ma, I'm still trying to get over the shock of you being gone. I still can't believe it. I don't think I need to pray for you, because I'm sure your soul will be given the royal treatment after the hell on earth you've been through. I'm so sorry you had to die alone in a place we had all grown to hate over the years. We would have been with you had we known. But maybe it was your choice to go this way.

I think I knew when I saw you three weeks ago that it would be the last time. You knew, too. I could see it in your eyes: the fight had finally left you. You probably saw it in my eyes, too. One thing I know for sure: you didn't die until you were ready. I'm going to miss you so much. I can't imagine my life without you in it. God bless you, Ma. I love you.

Real Life Lesson: While death may seem untimely, it comes precisely when it is due.

She Looks Good

When I returned to New York, Angela and I found ourselves in the same small office of the funeral director who had organized Martha and Tommy's services. We had developed a relationship with him that was akin to the one you have with your school principal: we would have done anything to avoid having to sit in his office!

We had to decide whether to have an open or a closed casket for Vita. Angela and I wanted it closed, just as we had for the other funerals but this time, we knew we couldn't. We knew that Vita would have wanted to be front and center as the hostess of her last party, and we feared the consequences of her wrath from "the other side" if we didn't respect her wishes. I had no doubt she was at least as strong in the spirit world as she was on earth.

By now, we were experts in the art of coffin shopping. We chose a rather elegant and expensive one for Vita that was lined in cream-colored satin with a beautiful dark lacquer finish on the outside. Vita had already told us what dress she wanted to be buried in: a hot pink chiffon gown with a sequined collar. She wanted to go out in style. We gave it to the funeral director, along with the matching shoes he requested, which made no sense to me. What did she need shoes for? He seemed thrilled to finally be given the opportunity to work his magic on a member of the Gisonni family.

I had reluctantly attended open-coffin wakes before and had always been perplexed by the comments people made about the appearance of the deceased. They would say something like, "Charlie looks great, doesn't he?" I used to think, How great can the guy look? He's dead! I would never be caught saying anything so absurd.

The funeral director asked Angela and me to arrive a few minutes early, to view Vita's body before the guests arrived. It was the last thing we wanted to do. The whole concept of viewing a dead body seemed morbid to us, but we got there early, just the same. From the back of the room, I could see the bright pink dress and Vita's flaming red hair. That was enough for me. I didn't want to get any closer.

The director beckoned us to come forward, from his post beside his masterpiece. Angela and I held each other's trembling hands and slowly walked to the front of the room. I felt like I was having an out-of-body experience, watching myself approach this coffin that contained my mother. I still couldn't believe she was dead. What if she popped up and said something to us? I certainly wouldn't put it past her!

When we got to the casket, we stared in amazement. Somehow, some way, this man had captured the old Vita, the pre-tumor Vita, erasing all the pain and sickness that had inhabited her face for the past ten years. My eyes must've bulged out of my head like a surprised cartoon character. I immediately turned to Angela without thinking and said, "She looks good!"

Despite our tears, we both started to chuckle. These contradicting emotions had become a familiar reaction to events over the last ten years. Somehow laughing inappropriately helped us through the pain. The director seemed pleased that we approved of his work, but our elation was probably a bit more than he'd expected.

I'm not sure if it was the jet lag, the hysteria, the unbearable pain of another loss or a combination of the above, but from the minute I walked into that room, the entire scene seemed surreal to me. All sorts of images filled my mind, like a collage of the last ten years sprinkled with trivial facts and faces.

With our hands clasped in front of us, we knelt in front of the casket to say a silent prayer. While I was looking at Vita and praying, I noticed something peculiar about her mouth. The corners of her thick, full lips were slightly upturned. Not only did she seem to be smirking, but her lips reminded me of the Joker from the movie *Batman*!

I turned to Angela and whispered, "What's with her lips? She looks like the Joker."

"Yeah," whispered Angela, "but she looks damn good."

Real Life Lesson: If we could only watch ourselves playing out this drama we call life on earth, some of the saddest moments would seem comical.

Laughter

We chose to reserve two days and nights for people to come and pay their respects to Vita at the funeral home. After the first day, Angela and I had a restless night at our old home. I figured Vita was getting even with us for laughing at her lips that day. Angela and I slept there alone. Joe was home in California, caring for our newly adopted puppies. On the second day of the wake, a priest was scheduled to deliver the eulogy before proceeding to the church.

Angela and I sat in the front row as the priest made his way up to the front of the room. Except for the occasional nose blower, there was dead silence. Everyone sat at attention, eyes on the priest, waiting for him to begin. We had never met him before but as soon as he started talking, it was obvious that English was his second language. Vita would have felt right at home, I thought. The first time he said her name, it sounded like "Rita" with a strong Indian accent. Angela and I looked at each other and then turned to the priest and quietly corrected him by whispering, "Vita."

The second time he mispronounced it, we started smirking. I'm not sure why we found this amusing but we did. Maybe because it's precisely when we're expected to be at our most serious and solemn that we experience a form of temporary insanity and act in the most irreverent ways.

The third time, when he said something that sounded like "Verita," Angela nudged me with her elbow and gave me her raised-eyebrow look. All of a sudden, I lost control.

My mind filled with images of embarrassing moments of laughter. I pictured the time I was ten and got caught laughing with my best friend during religious instruction classes. Then I suddenly remembered the famous Chuckles the Clown funeral episode on the *Mary Tyler Moore* show when Mary laughed hysterically while someone recited Chuckles' mantra: A little song, a little dance, a little seltzer down your pants.

My smirk quickly developed into a low giggle. I kept telling myself, "You're not going to laugh. You're not going to laugh." The more I thought about it, the more I couldn't control myself. The priest's words were fading into the background as the sound of my laughter became louder in my own head. By this time, Angela knew what was happening and instead of trying to calm me down, looked at me with a big grin. It was the kind of look that only sisters can give each other. There was no going back. I lost it!

I held my tissue up to my face to muffle the sound of my laughter. I kept hearing the priest's massacre of Vita's name and imagining those big red Joker lips, as if this were a skit on *Saturday Night Live.* Surely Vita would rise out of her coffin and give the priest and me a quick smack to the back of the head with the heel of one of her shoes! Aha, that's what she needed the shoes for! As my body shook uncontrollably with laughter and tears streamed down my face, I only hoped the people behind me assumed I was weeping.

By the time the priest was done, I felt terrible about laughing and showing such disrespect. At the same time, I felt totally exhilarated, as if the emotional weight of the past decade had suddenly been lifted from my soul. I had heard the expression "Laugh until you cry," but never "Cry until you laugh."

I suddenly realized that it didn't matter whether I was laughing or crying that day. The feeling was so intense that I got the same emotional release. Somehow, I knew Vita would understand. She may even have been laughing alongside me. After all, we had managed to laugh about a lot of things over the last ten years despite the tragic circumstances.

A week later, when my flight took off for California, I couldn't help but notice that the sky was a brilliant blue and the sun was shining bright. It was the most beautiful day in New York. I could even see a rainbow.

Dear God, I feel relieved that Ma is finally gone. With her death, so many problems are over, but while I prayed for this moment countless times before, I never imagined the incredible sense of loss. Vita, with all her ups and downs, was the mainstay of our lives. My heart is filled with a mixture of sadness, relief and joy. The overwhelming feeling is of calmness and peace. It's as if with one breath of wind, the storm is over and I have been safely and gently returned to shore.

Thank you for protecting me, for guiding me through the storm.

Real Life Lesson: Even at the most inappropriate moment, laughter has a tremendous healing power if your heart is in the right place.

A Moment in Time

Before Vita died, Joe and I adopted two Siberian Husky puppies and she had wasted no time letting me know how she felt. She thought it was a poor excuse for a family. She, of course, wanted grandchildren, the two-legged variety. We had only had Roxy and Bandit three weeks when Vita died. She couldn't know that one of them would very shortly teach me another lesson about life.

The day after I returned from Vita's funeral in New York, I learned that Roxy had genetically weak kidneys. The specialists told us she would never be house-trained, would have constant infections and would probably only live a year or two. The news hit me like a ton of bricks. Here I was thinking that all my problems were over and less than a week after Vita died, I was having conversations with a canine urologist about bladder control, antibiotics and death. It was as if Vita's problems had manifested themselves inside Roxy's body.

For a brief second I wondered how I was going to deal with all of this again. I didn't know if I had any fight left in me. Vita's passing was such a relief. I wanted a rest, but Roxy needed help and I was going to do whatever I could for her. Over the course of two years she endured several operations, hospital stays and months of rehabilitation (sound familiar?), but victory was sweet because she became a happy, healthy, house-trained member of our family whom we later nicknamed the Million Dollar Dog.

Roxy's ordeal showed me that our lives have no beginning and no end. Life and death are interwoven together, each a part of the other.

Angela, Joe and I moved on with our lives while the memories of our loved ones lived on in our hearts. When Angela did a final walk-through of Vita's house before selling it, she said that although it was completely empty of people and furniture, she could still see them as clear as day. Vita was in the kitchen, cooking. Dad was in his favorite chair, watching the news and rubbing Junior with his foot. Martha had just walked in the door from school, books in hand. And Aunt Yolanda was just about to call to say hello.

I kept a few items from all of them that will forever spark my memories and please my senses. A fedora hat in my closet has Dad's familiar scent to it. Aunt Yo's big lasagna pan evokes the many holiday gatherings we had together. Martha's spirit shines bright in the sparkling rubies from one of her rings. And could I forget Vita? She'd never allow it! My most treasured item of hers is a old dented ladle, which continually reminds me where my passion for cooking comes from. When I'm in my kitchen, I smell her kitchen, taste her food and sense her presence. And to Angela and me, a good piece of cake will always be *moistra*.

Life, death, family and tragedy are the oldest story lines around. My story could have been anyone's story. While it was happening, creating constant chaos and turmoil, turning my world upside down—and ultimately changing my perception of many things—it seemed to engulf the whole world. But seen in perspective, my family's ordeals were just a blip on Eternity's radar screen.

Real Life Lesson: Life never stops happening. Each ending marks a new beginning like a circle that continues forever.

Debbie (L) and Angela
1996

VI

REFLECTIONS

Playing Doctor

When I was nine years old, I wanted to be a doctor; not just any old doctor but a surgeon. I used to practice by carefully removing the plastic organ parts from the man in a game called Operation. Vita and Tommy were delighted with my interest in medicine and would have loved to have had a doctor in the family. Their generation suffered from the doctor-is-God complex. They held doctors in the highest esteem. Since they believed the doctor was always right, they never questioned the doctor's orders.

From the moment Vita's brain tumor was detected, our perception of doctors' abilities was constantly challenged. We quickly realized that the only people interested in Vita's health and well-being were herself and her family.

Vita suffered from headaches, dizziness and imbalance for two years before a brain CAT scan was finally ordered, and then only because I requested it. When her tumor was discovered, the doctors told us that she would be fully recovered in six weeks; after her operation, they told us she would never walk again.

Because we insisted on more physical therapy, she took her first steps two years later. Wearing steel braces on both legs from her hips to the bottom of her feet and holding on to two metal parallel bars for support, she took her first few awkward steps, making us weep for joy. Eventually, she was able to walk with the assistance of a quad cane (with four tips instead of one), a small calf brace on one leg, and a spotter (someone who walked alongside and steadied her).

When Vita's gag reflex hadn't improved weeks after surgery, the doctors instituted an indefinite "no food by mouth" policy as if they were prescribing two aspirins a day. They thought the nerves in her brain necessary for her gag reflex would never rejuvenate and that nothing proactive could be done. We continued to have faith that she would someday be able to eat again. We finally located a woman specialist who worked on restoring gag reflexes by strengthening the vocal cords through extensive vocal exercises.

By doing these exercises before meals, chewing her food slowly and swallowing on one side, Vita was able to eat soft baby food within weeks, and solids within months. This was after not having eaten by mouth for three years. She was able to taste food again only because we pursued options beyond the doctors' recommendations. Although her gag reflex was never perfect and the risk of pneumonia from food or liquid entering her lungs was always there, we decided the quality of her life was more important.

Lifetime confinement to a hospital was another recommendation we were not willing to accept. We knew that a nursing home environment would slowly kill Vita's spirit and will to live. She needed to be home. With the help of home health-care agencies and persistent calls to insurance companies, persuading them that 24-hour home nursing care would be less expensive, she came home three years after her operation. Once again, we prevailed.

Overall, we found women doctors more open to trying things outside the sphere of conventional Western medicine. They were more compassionate, more informative and less threatened by our knowledge. Many of their male counterparts did not like to have their territory invaded and would spit out a bunch of seemingly smart, actually incoherent answers.

The sad thing about this behavior is that most patients accept it, feel stupid and walk away with their tails between their legs. Not us!

We decided that there was no educational degree in the world that gave someone a license to be arrogant and·condescending, or to intimidate another person. We refused to tolerate it. We probed; we made suggestions; we phoned relentlessly until we got the answers we deserved as human beings, realizing in the process that the doctor himself was only human. He did not have all the answers. In fact, sometimes he had the wrong answers.

Within months of being thrown into contact with the medical industry, the once foreign world of strange acronyms started to make sense to us. We used the medical jargon so comfortably that the doctors began thinking we were doctors.

Vita also got a medical education. She could instruct the best of nurses on any of her regularly required medical procedures, step by step. These included such routines as replacing a stomach tube after it had burst, preparing breathing treatments, and suctioning mucous out of her lungs. She took great pride in breaking in and training new nurses. Not bad for a person with an eighth-grade education.

I vividly remember the time she learned about "blood gas" after she had been rushed to emergency because of difficulty breathing. The doctors took a blood test to determine whether she had enough oxygen or too much carbon dioxide in her system.

She heard one doctor say, "Her gas is too high."

Vita, thinking he was talking about flatulence, quickly responded, "Oh no, I don't have any gas."

Amid this life-threatening situation in a chaotic emergency room, we all started laughing as the doctor explained to her what he meant by gas. From that time forward, she was able to interpret her own gas numbers, immediately knowing if the range was too high or too low.

In addition to doctors and specialists, we got to know many of the nurses working hospital shifts or providing home health-care. They tended to be more compassionate and better able to understand the patients' emotional needs than the doctors. But they, too, were only human, and the combination of understaffed hospitals and long shifts created a breeding ground for mistakes.

On one occasion, a hospital nurse poured a dose of liquid medicine into Vita's tracheotomy tube that was intended to go into her stomach tube. Fortunately, I was visiting her at the time and knew something was terribly wrong when her chest and lungs started burning up. I quickly ran to the nurses' station and explained the problem. The head nurse, who immediately knew that a mistake had been made, summoned three people to help flush out Vita's lungs. I shudder to think what could have happened if I hadn't been there. I read an article a few years ago that said medical errors kill more Americans than traffic accidents, breast cancer or AIDS.

I believe many medical professionals instituted a "Don't ask, don't tell" policy well before the military. Thanks to the Internet, ordinary people now have access to information previously only available to physicians, allowing patients to take control of their own health and the decisions affecting it. The doctors who continue to treat educated patients as their worst nightmare will have to change the way they conduct their business in the new millennium.

Real Life Lesson: The doctor is not God. Ask every question and question every answer.

The Grass Isn't Always Greener

When disaster strikes close to home or heart, the most natural reaction is to think that you and only you have been dealt the worst hand of fate in all of history. Of course, on the surface, that sounds irrational but it's precisely how most people feel. When Vita was first diagnosed, I had this typically myopic view. If she had completely recovered in six weeks, as originally expected, my focus would never have expanded beyond her hospital room, and I would never have realized how lucky we were.

It was only after years of Vita's illness that my perception of my family's multiple crises changed. I became aware of all the other sick people in those hospitals. The people in pain, the people with no visitors, the people who yelled, the people who were insane, the people who died. The people who lived but couldn't speak, walk, breathe, eat, see, hear or move. The people with no arms or legs!

I became aware how fortunate Vita was not to have been given a worse fate. There was always someone who was suffering more than she was. I felt deep compassion for their families because I knew they looked upon us with envy just as we had looked upon others the same way. "If she could only eat," we thought, "or walk, or breathe normally, then everything would be okay." But we were stuck with what we had and that forced us to look beyond our own troubles.

The belief that happiness can be attained if only you have one more thing has permeated every aspect of human life from the beginning of time. It keeps everyone wanting more, whether it's money, possessions or power. It's a vicious cycle of greed that never ends and never produces satisfaction.

Vita's illness opened my eyes to the hundreds of people who would have traded their problems for hers in a second. Instead of feeling sorry for my family, I began to feel grateful for what we had. I became more aware of all the suffering that's going on in the world, not just my own.

Real Life Lesson: Be grateful for who you are or are not, what you can or can't do, what you have or don't have. These are your personal blessings in this lifetime.

Small World

When Vita arrived from Italy, her family, like most European immigrants of the 1940s, settled in a neighborhood with other Western Europeans like themselves. Many who came from small villages had never ventured more than a couple of miles away from home before they came to the United States. Once here, they created their own communities, which separated them from other cultures and races. When Angela and I attended public school in the Bronx, we interacted with people of all colors, but there was an underlying understanding that they were not part of our home environment. After Vita came home from the hospital, all of that changed.

The people whom Vita relied on for care and companionship at home were people of every race, color and creed. They were Jewish, African-American, Cuban, Haitian, Peruvian, Filipino, Asian and Puerto Rican. They dressed, bathed and befriended her; cooked, laughed and fought with her. While virtually confined to her own home, she learned more about the world than when crossing the Atlantic Ocean between two continents.

She was introduced to everything from potato pancakes to voodoo, from cornrows to Buddha. And she reciprocated by teaching her nurses and aides about her own culture, beliefs and cuisine. The people who were once strangers became part of our extended family and we became part of theirs—sharing birthdays, holidays and our life together.

The funniest moments in this rich cultural mix arose out of the exchanges between Vita and her nurses, particularly those whose first language was also not English. The world of medicine opened up a whole new area of vocabulary for Vita that she immediately corrupted. Since *oxygen* was too difficult for her, she renamed it *auction*. She referred to her portable asthma inhaler as "the puff," and when the nurses administered her nebulizing breathing treatment, Vita would say she was "smoking the pipe." I loved watching the expression on a new nurse's face when Vita told her it was time to smoke the pipe.

Vita's verbal idiosyncrasies and some of the nurses' own struggles with English made conversations in the house sound like a United Nations meeting. Although the objective was not world peace, having the common goal of Vita's well-being allowed her and her nurses to transcend their differences of language, culture and race.

After Vita died, we kept in touch with some of those nurses who had become part of our family for a very short time, sometimes just weeks. They had all moved on to different jobs by then and vanished from our lives as if they'd been sent down from heaven to do a job and left when it was over. The fact that we didn't stay in touch doesn't diminish their impact on our family during that time. We are forever grateful for what they did.

Real Life Lesson: Sometimes you need to be face to face with life and death to realize we are all more alike than different.

Prejudice Has Many Faces

Although Italian was their native language, Vita and Tommy made a conscious decision to speak only English to us. Angela was born in 1958, a time of Americanism. Our parents didn't want us to suffer the labeling and discrimination they encountered as Italian-Americans. They wanted American children who could have their American dreams fulfilled. Unfortunately, their strong desire to fit into the American culture, combined with their intense fear of prejudice, resulted in their children's not learning a second language.

Differences in race, language and nationality are common targets for discrimination, but prejudice has many faces. Anything different about a person can excite other people's prejudice. That's what happens to the disabled. Most of them don't look normal according to society's guidelines.

Vita's physical attributes changed drastically in the years following her operation. Her body became thin and frail, except for her belly, which was swollen with excess air from her stomach tube. She was slumped over in her wheelchair and a metal brace hugged her right leg from the knee down.

The red plastic button that plugged her tracheotomy opening looked like something out of a science fiction movie. It had to be uncorked repeatedly during the day for breathing treatments, suctioning or coughing up phlegm that accumulated in her lungs. Not a pleasant sight for the squeamish!

These unfortunate characteristics were accompanied by the uncoordinated movements and limited dexterity caused by misfiring brain signals. Often her right arm would move in exact symmetry with her left. When she consciously moved her left arm, her brain told both arms to move in the exact same pattern. It was amusing to watch and became a great conversation piece for new visitors!

We were so accustomed to seeing Vita's quirky deformities on a regular basis that they became normal to us. She was still the same person she had always been. We would even poke fun at the medical procedures, sometimes administering them ourselves, while imitating the slurping sound of the suctioning machine or the gurgling of her stomach. When we took her out in public and behaved this way, stares and whispers snapped us back to reality and reminded us of how different Vita now looked, moved and sounded.

Prejudice isn't limited to name-calling and acts of violence. Before Vita was sick, I used to turn the other way when I saw a disabled person, placing them in a box outside of my world, as if they were invisible. They were beyond my comfort zone, so I didn't acknowledge their existence. That simple act of ignoring a person is a form of discrimination. It says, "I'm not looking at you because you disturb me. You're inferior to me. I can't see or hear you. You have no feelings." Once I saw how this type of treatment hurt Vita, I understood what prejudice meant and how it felt.

Who's to say what's normal and acceptable appearance and what's not? Normality is relative. As bad as Vita looked, there were places like rehab centers where her condition was the best in the room. Once I took the time to talk to physically disabled people, I saw beyond the surface of their bodies and guess what? They have the same needs, feelings and desires as any human being. They're not contagious, inferior or dumb. They're courageous people who really need those handicapped parking spaces. (Just in case you're ever tempted!)

Vita's disabilities showed me how much I took for granted. I saw how the slightest change in a person's body could make performing the simplest task an arduous process. I couldn't imagine getting through a day without the use of my dominant hand. That loss, small compared to Vita's, would cause havoc in my life, making everyday activities such as writing, cooking or even wiping my butt nearly impossible. Eventually my pride and self-confidence would erode.

Fifteen percent of the U.S. population is disabled, due to chronic health conditions and impairments. I don't ignore them anymore. I look them in the eye. I give them a friendly smile. I talk to them. I open the door for them. How hard could it be for everyone to do the same? It's not a big deal but it makes a big difference.

Real Life Lesson: Being in a seemingly better situation in life than someone else doesn't make you a better person.

It's Just a Job

During the time my family troubles went from bad to worse, my career went full-steam ahead. I was beginning to think my promotions at work were tied to deaths in my family. Right after Martha died, I was promoted to regional sales manager. During Tommy's last days I became associate publisher. Three weeks before Vita died, I was promoted to the top spot, publisher of a magazine. I wasn't sure if I should be grateful that these promotions kept my mind off my family situation or spooked that the next one would claim another life!

Just as I had been offered the job in California as my family's troubles in New York started to multiply, each of my new jobs seemed to come at a time when I needed an emotional reprieve. It was as if I had a guardian angel who kept balancing the lowest depths of my grieving with the highest achievements of my career. And because I kept them emotionally separated, I was quite adept at shifting gears. When I was with my family, I was one hundred percent committed to their world and their needs, and when I was in work mode, I had as intense a drive and passion for that.

In 1994, when I became a publisher, the magazine I took over was in a state of turmoil. The previous publisher had abruptly left, taking half the existing staff with him. Industry rumors that the magazine was folding were rampant. Internal morale was at an all-time low, causing more departures every day. It was my job to turn it all around, rebuild the team and start moving in a positive direction. My name and reputation were on the line, along with my future career.

One day, a fellow publisher who was much more experienced than I was asked me, "Debbie, I just don't get it. How can you be so calm and focused when everything around you is crumbling?"

I laughed. "This stuff is nothing," I said. "This is not important enough to be stressed about. There are no lives at stake here. If you want to talk about something stressful, something worth losing control over, I'll tell you a story about losing four members of my family in four years. Now that's stress!"

That conversation often reminded me of something I was told by one of my favorite bosses early in my career: It's just a job.

Real Life Lesson: Make work a part of your life, not life a part of your work.

Coping

When I tell my story to people, they look at me in disbelief and wonder how I got through it all and came out of it a stable, happy, grounded person. I even asked myself the same question as I was writing this book. My first inclination was to say, I don't know how I got through it, I just did. You take each situation day by day and get through it. While you're in it, you don't think about *how*. But on further reflection, I found that I used many coping mechanisms that seemed to come naturally. I hope these will help you realize that you, too, can get through anything.

Do Something

It's very easy to sit back when you're in a terrible situation and feel defeated. In fact, it's almost comforting to know that there isn't anything you can do, that it's out of your control. Then you can feel sorry for yourself. On the other hand, immersing yourself in the situation and doing something about it is actually a coping mechanism. By creating solutions, you are coping. In other words, stop whining and start doing. You may not be able to tackle the entire problem but it's usually the little things that count the most.

Be Optimistic

I think anyone can learn how to be optimistic. This is a personality trait I've always had. I'm the one who always sees the glass as being half full and convinces others it is as well! I try to make the best of bad situations, no matter how horrible people think they are. This ability has followed me in everything I ever did in my personal and professional life. If you look hard enough, you can find the silver lining to every difficulty. You just have to be willing to look! I *never* believed things would get continually worse in my family. And although they did, it was the small victories along the way that I clung to. And since I could not predict the future, I chose to believe that something better was around the corner, rather than something worse. After all, there's a fifty-fifty chance, isn't there? Anything is possible!

Have Faith

Faith allows you to give up control and responsibility in a way which helps you cope. I've stated that I believe in a God who is all good and all love and I believe God helps us on our journey. Each of us has a different journey in life. I cannot change someone else's path. I can only help them accept and move along it. I believe this journey is part of a master road map for each of our lives, an agreement we made in spirit before we entered this lifetime. An agreement that is forgotten when we take on bodily form. Faith allows me to say, "What's meant to be, is meant to be. It is what it is, and I am what I am." It allows me to surrender to something greater than me and life itself. It allows me to believe that things work out for the best—the way they are supposed to work out. It is faith that allows me to believe that death is just an illusion.

Pray or Meditate

Never underestimate the power of prayer and meditation. Not only will you benefit, but your prayers can help every other creature on earth. It makes no difference what your religious beliefs are or whether you choose to pray by yourself or with others. Prayer and meditation are just forms of communication that connect your inner power to the power of the universe. In prayer, you are talking. In meditation, you are listening. This is your personal link or lifeline to God, the Creator, however you define it. Amidst all the turmoil in my life, it was prayer and meditation that quieted my soul and made me feel like I was not alone. That was the best therapy I could ever have. I continue these conversations with God and my angels every day.

Learn to Love

I was particularly lucky to have entered this world with a sufficient respect and love for myself. I wasn't always the prettiest or the smartest or the winner, but I always felt special in some way and that's what made me like and love myself. Given that, I could freely give love to other people. In fact, I love to love people! I generally like everyone I meet. Not in a sexual way but in a human connection way. I admire most people for whatever special traits they have and I like to tell them so! I believe that when you send messages like that into the world, you get back that same love, tenfold. You naturally attract it. When you have love in your life, problems become that much more palatable. There is no power in the universe greater than love. Accept it thankfully and return it unconditionally.

Have a Diversion

Everyone needs a distraction, something that diverts their energy in a positive way. While the work schedule I kept might not have been the healthiest, it was what I needed at the time: something in my life I could entirely control, where my actions produced positive results. It balanced the other part of my life, which was haywire! My job fed my ego and my sense of self worth. For someone else, another diversion such as a hobby, a child or a sport might work. You need something that takes your mind off that all-consuming problem and allows you to put it in perspective.

Accept What You Can't Control

This is probably one of most important ways both Joe and I got through it all. This is how Joe coped with it all. His basic attitude was that you must accept what you can't change and change what you can. Where I had always wanted complete control, he taught me to let go of things I couldn't control. So I didn't beat myself up emotionally about stuff I couldn't change, but I changed everything I could with a vengeance. I got rid of attachments to any specific outcome because that only set me up for disappointment. I came up with creative solutions which allowed me some control over the situation. This, in turn, helped me cope. Although I could not extinguish the entire fire, I could cool it down a few degrees by putting out a few flames, which made it more bearable. So I did!

Remember Your Inner Strength

This is an important characteristic in every aspect of life, but when you're faced with big challenges it becomes even more important. This goes hand-in-hand with integrity and not giving up on anything or any-one you believe in. If you don't have basic principles to hold on to like a life raft, you'll drift and drown. Strength of character means knowing that the decision you made is the right one and you're going to stick by it. This keeps you going no matter what. This is your inner foundation.

Find the Humor

It's so important not to take yourself or life's mishaps too seriously. If you do, you fail to find the humor in everything that happens and there is always humor to be found. You just have to be willing to look for it. Once you take things less seriously, problems are easier to deal with. Some of us are born with a better sense of humor than others. I don't think I really tapped into any sense of humor until all this happened. I was a pretty serious child.

Move On

In life we tend to hang onto the past even though rationally we know we cannot change what has happened. We dwell on the negative and then it ends up dwelling on us—our spirit, our attitude, our outlook. The past represents baggage that drags us down and I've always hated baggage. I let go of bad moments, bad decisions and bad people like so many hot potatoes. I hate to rewind, to go backwards. I never regret. I just move on, because I know that whatever it is I'm concerned about will pass. Time is always on your side if you allow yourself to move with it.

There is no instruction manual for life. No troubleshooting guide. No test at the end to determine if you learned all the right stuff. Everyone is dealt a unique set of cards. How you play them is up to you. All you can hope to accomplish by the end of the game is to have lived your life from a foundation of love, learned from every experience and inspired others to do the same.

Real Life Lesson: No matter what challenges Life hands you, you have the power within to triumph.

Debbie and Joe with
Roxy, Bandit and Shadow (L-R)
1999

Prayer of Thanks

Dear God, thank you for my life on this earth and all its challenges. Thank you for giving me free will to love and be loved, to make my own decisions, to learn from my own mistakes, to laugh when I am happy, to cry when I am sad. Thank you for my family, my friends, my pets, my colleagues and for every other living creature I meet along my journey. Thank you for giving me strength to overcome adversity, to do what's right for the benefit of the greater good, to rise above negativity. Thank you for giving me hope that there will be an end to all suffering and the beginning of a world filled with light and everlasting love.

About the Author

Debbie Gisonni is Founder and President of Real Life Lessons™, a company dedicated to serving women in business, people who have lost a loved one, or those who have experienced a major change in their lives. For fifteen years Debbie held top executive positions in the high-tech magazine publishing industry in Silicon Valley. She left a lucrative career (stock options and all) to write the book *Vita's Will*: a story about dealing with the deaths of four family members in four years and the most important life lessons she learned in the process.

Currently Debbie is President of the San Francisco chapter of the Women's National Book Association. She also volunteers for organizations that teach teenage girls business and life skills. As an experienced speaker, she has addressed executives, marketing, sales and advertising managers in corporate America, and is available to speak to women's groups, business organizations and cancer/suicide/health care support groups. Debbie's signature talk is called, "Real life lessons you can't live without."

Originally from New York, Debbie currently lives in the San Francisco Bay Area with her husband and their Siberian Huskies. Contact her through reallifelessons.com or PMB #396, 1017 El Camino Real, Redwood City, CA 94063-1632.

Ten percent of the author's proceeds from this book will be donated to the following institutions: Y-me National Breast Cancer Organization, National Brain Tumor Foundation, International Myeloma Foundation and the American Foundation for Suicide Prevention.